Goireann Beirt Bóthar

"Two Shorten the Road"

Ancient Gaelic Proverb

can you Believe it !

Deirdre G. Maguire

Copyright ©2016 by Deirdre Maguire

All rights reserved. This book or any portion thereof may not be reproduced or used in any manner whatsoever without the express written permission of the publisher, except for the use of brief quotations in a book review.

First Printing, 2016

ISBN-13: 978-1539535966
ISBN-10: 1539535967

62 Middle Tollymore Rd.
Newcastle, BT33 0JJ
Northern Ireland
United Kingdom

www.deirdremaguire.com

can you Believe it !

INTRODUCTION
How it all came about

By Deirdre G. Maguire

There I was, searching in the Habilitat* library for something that would inspire and encourage me.

Our now bi-annual FasterEFT Habilitat marathon complete, I had decided to stay on for a few days to do some extra work and also enjoy the company of the sweet souls who are the residents there.

The buzz of anticipation in the lead up to the marathon is palpable and transformations during it are phenomenal. Secrets are unburdened. Hurts are released. Lives are changed. There is nothing quite like the experience. Not for nothing is Habilitat known as the Place of Change; and regarding my own personal journey, now was no exception!

This time it took the form of a book. As I scanned the shelves I came on one that was to help me so much over the next few months. Comprised of stories about people who had turned their lives around in adversity, I scanned the first one and knew that this was what I needed.

With permission from Jeff Nash, the director, I borrowed the book; and every night, I would ration myself by reading one story. During that challenging leg of what I now call my journey back to me, those stories gave me hope, encouraged me to hang in there and keep tapping until, gradually,

I regained the emotional grip on my life.
And then I had the idea …

What if I could hand my clients a book of inspirational stories based on all the testimonials I'd heard from my work with clients around the globe?

What you are holding/reading right now is a result of that thought!

Perhaps the greatest part of any personal challenge is the feeling of being alone. Looking down the barrel of the emotional gun of cancer certainly felt like that for me. Learning how others had survived countless kinds of other challenges was a lifeline to me. That's why I created this book.

The purpose of CAN YOU BELIEVE IT ! is to provide comfort, encouragement and inspiration for those who can currently see no relief. Stepping into the personal world of ordinary people and walking with them as they overcome extraordinary challenges is one of the most empowering gifts you can give yourself

Contrary to the old conditioned belief that vulnerability is weakness, the world is crying out for openness, exposure and authenticity. Accounts like these carry a very powerful message to the unconscious. If you do not know about the power of the unconscious now, you will by the end of these recollections.

This book is a Powerhouse, packed full of the emotional juice that can pull us through our challenges. As I say to all my clients - whether in my talks, my workshops, my 3-day private intensives, or in personal sessions -

can you Believe it !

anywhere in the world, our stories may be different but the pain is the same. In truth, we are all one. So if you picked up this book for the same reason as me that day in that Habilitat library, I invite you to roll your emotional sleeves up.

Embark upon your personal journey.

Know that you are never alone.

If I could do it, if they could do it...

You can do it too.

Peace always
Deirdre x

* Drugs and Alcohol rehabilitation Facility

Be not afraid of Life.

Believe that life is worth living

and your belief

will help create the fact.

William James

can you Believe it !

DEDICATION

Dedicated to you, gentle Eileen,
my first beautiful client friend.

Thank you for teaching me that it's okay
to become quiet enough to listen;
then courageous enough to live by my own truth.

Acknowledgement

I am so delighted to have this opportunity to publicly acknowledge those who have helped and supported me in bringing another part of my dream into reality.

I begin by acknowledging my immediate family: My mum (affectionately known as my wee mummy!), my brothers and sisters Brian, Denise, Paul and Marcella, their partners past and present, and all my beautiful, gorgeous, multi-talented nieces and nephews . Words cannot express how much I love each and every one of you. Thank you for all the ways you continue to support me, including putting up with my incessant passion for this work!

To my extended family, aunts uncles and cousins on both sides, especially my Aunt Philomena and Uncle John in New York, whose welcome and support is always there and whose home-made wheaten bread is legendary!

To my friend, Sharon for never doubting me and for taking care of my wee friend Lucky when it had to happen.

(From Lucky, a big thanks to you too, Jackie x)

To my (SoCal) Californian friends (and you know who you are!)I love you. Thank you for all the love I receive, and thank you for being there-even through the biggest challenges.

To my very precious local community in Newcastle, for all the ways you ask how I'm doing, and encourage and support me to keep moving this work forward.

To Robert Smith, Founder of FasterEFT, my mentor and fellow earth angel (don't tell him I said that - far too woo-woo!), thank you for the time you invested in me. Thank you for your friendship. Thank you for the best morning coffee. Thank you for (most of, but not all) your jokes. And more than anything, thank you for your love.

To my FasterEFT family, whose unfailing support has allowed this book to be here.

To Jeff Nash, and my brothers and sisters at Habilitat, thank you for welcoming me home without question when, in order to survive, I knew I had to leave mine. Thank you for your respect. Thank you for unwittingly pulling me into shape, and thank you all for the vital life lessons you have given me. Mahalo.

To those who have supported me by helping to bring my workshops to life (and you know who you are!) I am forever grateful. Thank you!

To all my clients who placed their faith in me by rolling up their emotional sleeves to do their work, I humbly bow to your courage.

To all those who took the time and showed their faith in myself and my work by writing their stories for this book – what can I say – without you there would be no book! From the bottom of my heart, thank you!

To Margherita, Odille, Paula and Campbell, whose loyalty and attention to detail is helping to bring this whole dream into reality, thank you so much.

And of course, thank you to you, the reader. Keep going for your dream. It's right there waiting for you …

Finally, I want to say thank you to you, daddy my darling father. Without you, none of us would be reading this.

For everything it was your journey to go through, I thank you. For the message you carried and continue to carry, I thank you. For everything you taught me to do or not to do, I thank you.

For the certainty of your love I keep safely in my heart, I thank you.

For every life you've saved by giving yours,
I thank you.
I miss you
I love you.

Peace always,
Deirdre x

Foreword

By Robert G. Smith

FasterEFT exists because I was looking for a way to help my wife. I figured if I could solve her problems, all our problems would be solved. Of course, it doesn't work that way; and, although I didn't know it, I had just as many problems as she did!

Little did I know back then that this was the start of the journey that would lead to the powerful transformative modality that is FasterEFT as we know it today. Over the twenty odd years since, there have been hundreds of thousands of accounts from those who have used FasterEFT to transform their lives; and I'm excited that Deirdre has created this sample of inspiring success stories so that you can see what's possible for you.

FasterEFT is a self-empowering modality based on a formidable thinking system that you can use to completely change your life. As you'll see from the stories in this book, it can work on anything.

Let these stories give you the inspiration, encouragement and vision of what you can achieve. And then I invite you take the steps yourself.

Use the FasterEFT process persistently to see the results you're looking for. Notice that although the people in this book have had to overcome many, varied challenges, their common theme is their determination.

I often say that the most important tool you have is persistence. It is persistence that enabled me to find out everything I could about how the mind works. It is persistence that allowed me to combine the best of all of the modalities I studied and create what we now know as FasterEFT. And it is that same persistence that has enabled Deirdre to produce this book.

Since I've known her, I have watched Deirdre progress from a low point in her life to the empowered, strong, successful woman I am proud to call my friend today. She's been through some intense life challenges, which you'll read about in her story. But her persistence in using FasterEFT and her commitment to taking responsibility for her own life got her through those challenges. She is now even stronger and more of her 'authentic self' today.

I first met Deirdre in 2009, when she invited me to speak to a small gathering of friends and family at her home in Northern Ireland. She was also one of the 12 attendees at my very first international weeklong FasterEFT training seminar, in Oklahoma City.

She was right there with me when I brought the first team to Habilitat. She was the one I asked to work with Jeff Nash, the Director, to help him release old patterns of addiction that, despite having being clean and sober for years, were nonetheless still alive inside him. He too has contributed his success story.

From client and student to colleague, Deirdre has also become my close ally and dearest friend, and I am honored to have been a part of her healing journey. Deirdre helped me take FasterEFT around the world, and, on a personal level, we've covered some miles together too!

Now a FasterEFT Master Practitioner, author, speaker, and trainer with countless client successes, she makes me proud - especially when I think about how far she has come.

In this book, you have been given a powerful opportunity. As you read it, notice how these ordinary people have achieved extraordinary changes in their lives, and allow yourself to be inspired and encouraged in what YOU can achieve!

I'm excited that Deirdre is sharing this inspiration with the world, and I'm also excited for you as you make the most of the opportunity you've been given to truly empower yourself to create the life you really want.

FasterEFT is a result of my persistence. This book is a result of Deirdre's persistence. Now use your own persistence to take this gift and make the most of it for your own life.

Peace,

Robert G. Smith
Founder of FasterEFT

CONTENTS

INTRODUCTION i

DEDICATION vii

Acknowledgement.. ix

Foreword xiii

You Have Come to this Book for a Reason 1

Letter to My Daughter- the Unwritten Contract of Parenting 7

Oh, What a Beautiful Mornin' 19

What's Wrong with Me? 27

I Didn't Have Huge Traumas 39

You're Not Dying Now 53

No Longer a Victim 65

The Power to Heal Was Mind the Whole Time! 69

The Business Comes First 79

Never Give Up! 85

Opening the Door to the World of the Mind 93

Keep it Light and Make Them Laugh! 101

Drugs Were My Best Friend 109

From Riches – to Homeless – to Peace 113

My Thoughts Were Responsible for My Weight Issues 125

From Stressed to Success..133

I Don't Need to be Invisible Anymore 141

I Help People Feel Good... It's That Simple! 153

My Journey to Serenity, Healing and Balance 161

I Was Desperate to Have Someone in My Life 169

You Are Never Too Old to Learn 177

I Wished I'd Never Heard of FasterEFT!...185

FasterEFT and Financial Transformation 193

My Daughter's Cancer, FasterEFT, and a $120,000+ Hospital Bill 201

I Didn't Know if My Dreams Were Really Possible 207

IT Was the Best Session I Ever Had 211

From Mr. Mom to Global Stress Expert 217

A Nurse's Recovery 223

I Learned to Ask for Help 231

I Was Born to be Doing This Work 243

Heal Me or Kill Me, God 249

Conclusion...257

What's the Next Step? 259

More from Deirdre Maguire 261

PHP Self Mastery Pillars of Truth..263

can you Believe it !

You Have Come to this Book for a Reason

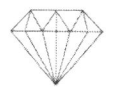

Adam Gray

Ever since I was little I have had a keen interest in what I now know to be called 'personal growth.' I believe that we can be, do, or have anything that we want. We all have dreams and goals, but, unfortunately for most of us, our dreams and goals pass us by and we never really 'get there.'

FasterEFT has helped me in many ways. During my childhood, I was always very shy. If I was asked to stand up in front of the class, I would instantly go bright red and be very embarrassed. Over the years, little did I know that I was building upon the issue by adding more and more 'resources' (as we sometimes refer to 'memories' in FasterEFT) to support the problem. As I got older, I found it very difficult to be in large groups. I would remain very quiet and wouldn't interact with anybody.

FasterEFT has allowed me to work through all of the resources that were supporting my shyness and totally 'flip' (or transform) those memories. I love the 'flipping' part. I find it absolutely incredible how we can take the charge out of the memories and then flip them to a positive. As I write this, it almost seems as if I am making the story up about the shyness. The reason for this is because once we change the memories, we cannot see them the same way again. So as I write this, I cannot help but wonder, 'Was

I ever really that shy?'

Today I am able to do things I never dreamed I could do at one stage of my life. Now, I love social events, and I am often the centre of the party. It isn't unusual to see me singing in front of many people in my yellow Freddie Mercury jacket - or making the whole room laugh! And in my career as a digital marketing manager, I have given presentations to universities and businesses. I attend conferences with thousands of other people and travel all over England, meeting people I've never met before. I have even been filmed giving an interview about my professional expertise in digital hosting, platforms, and web development.

> Today my blood pressure is perfect,
> and the only change I've made is to use FasterEFT.

Over the years I have seen incredible improvements in my health. At one point, my blood pressure was very high. The doctor advised that if this situation were to continue, I would need to be put on medication. Today my blood pressure is perfect, and the only change I've made is to use FasterEFT. My diet and exercise level are no different.

I believe the mind is a very powerful tool and that our beliefs about us and the world hold the key to achieving our dreams and goals. I have studied many different techniques that help to change our beliefs, and I have discovered powerful tools we all can use to help achieve our dreams and goals. I have read countless books, tested tools, applied techniques, and studied with many well-known personal growth teachers.

I have since come to learn that we are all on a journey - a journey through life - and we all came here to do great things. Unfortunately, so many of us don't ever achieve our goals, and we give in to the opinions of others - to criticism! We are told that it is best to stay as we are and that it isn't safe to expand, to grow, to develop, or to achieve.

There are countless stories of those that have changed the world and overcome criticisms or rejections, such as Henry Ford of the Ford Motor Company and the Wright brothers who developed and piloted the first airplane. All the personal growth teachers I have studied have taught me about the power of the mind and how we can live our dream life, but I believe there is a missing key to truly unlock your full potential, and the missing key is FasterEFT.

I describe FasterEFT as a healing technique, a 'trance breaker,' and a belief system. FasterEFT stands for 'faster emotionally focused transformation,' and that's exactly what it is. It's a technique that delivers faster transformation by focusing on our emotions to break the 'trances' that are no longer required and could be limiting our growth.

How did I learn about FasterEFT? It was strictly by coincidence one day in the year 2008. I was browsing YouTube and was instantly captured by Robert Smith's character. His unique nature and easy-to-understand way with words kept me glued to the computer screen. I knew that this guy was onto something, and I just knew I had to learn this technique. I decided to make an investment in me, and I bought the complete DVD, at-home training course.

Then I decided to put the technique to the test and have sessions with certified FasterEFT practitioners. I have since worked with practitioners all over the world, and, in addition to benefitting from the FasterEFT process, have made some very good friends. I would like to take this opportunity to say a special thank you to my partner Carl for his long standing support and for allowing me to shine and to my Spiritual Teacher, Gail Jefferson, at FasterEFT Spa (www.fastereftspa.com). I will forever be grateful for Gail's dedication, friendship, patience, and caring nature. Combining my interest in digital marketing and my passion in personal growth, I decided to create my own personal development blog. Many FasterEFT practitioners have their own natural way of helping people to become the best of themselves, and my way is in the form of providing informative, helpful, and life-changing content to the world using my blog.

If you haven't tried FasterEFT yet, then please do. It works! Before I found FasterEFT to combat my limiting beliefs, I tried many techniques. And while there are lots of techniques that made me feel more relaxed and focused, it was always for the short term, because the limiting beliefs still existed. FasterEFT is for me, my life changer. In fact, I believe it is the missing ingredient in the Law of Attraction.

Once you clear the negative beliefs,
you will naturally attract better things

We can try to think and feel as best we can to attract what we desire, but unless you deal with the limiting beliefs hidden in the subconscious mind, then it's going to be a difficult time. The great thing about FasterEFT is that once you clear the negative beliefs, you will naturally attract better things.

The universe is on your side, and you have come across this book for a reason.

The universe is on your side, and you have come across this book for a reason. I would like to leave you with some final words . . .

Whatever you would like freedom from, start to make that change in this very moment. Take a deep breath and understand that you are in the right place and you have found the right technique. Things can be different and better! FasterEFT has changed my life. My wish is that it changes yours. Peace.

Adam M. Gray ACIM

Digital Marketing Manager, Wordpress Website Developer and Personal Development Blogger.

Website:
www.adammarcgray.com

Letter to My Daughter- the Unwritten Contract of Parenting

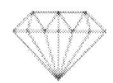

Arlene

A Note to the Reader from Deirdre Maguire:

This beautiful true story from my client who became a friend takes the form of a letter from herself to the miracle that is her newly born daughter. FasterEFT spans 3 generations as it frees Arlene from the grief of her mother's untimely death - and gives her the courage to face the many challenges that come with growing into (and being) a new mum.

Peace always, Deirdre

The unwritten contract of parenting.

Dear Heidi,

WOW! I can barely believe it! You are just perfect, perfect THE WAY YOU ARE! Not that saccharine sweet 'pretty in pink,' princess-type thing that others may try to force-feed to you. But you are perfect, perfect in YOUR design, for your life that lies ahead of you. *(By the way, we will revisit the princess thing in a few years!)*

You should know that you are my greatest love.

That doesn't mean that I love Daddy any less of course - trust me he would say the same. That's part of the unwritten contract of parenting, for that IS the correct order of things – that your child is your greatest love.
The universe deems it to be so.

The same universe that brought you to us . . . That when WE were ready, YOU were ready too. That when I had healed my heart enough, you were willing to get beating - enough so that from my experiences, from the skills that I have now learned, you swung your way to us - and boy, have you made you mark! An awesome one!

I'm so sure about this perfect timing that, in fact, it feels like you and Grandma (my own mum) sat there plotting. Yes, I see Grandma with a cheeky 'knowing' grin on her face. Yeah, I'm pretty sure she wrote the 'brief' to God for you. I am thinking she might have even asked for it like a recipe for the most wonderful thing in the world:

Ingredients List for Heidi by Grandma:

Must be very active – Mum needs to keep fit. (Baby must be able to out-run Mum at suitable age.)

Must talk LOTS. (This child needs to be able to hold her own in this family – my god, can they talk.)

Must be able to climb everywhere. (Mum will want her to have a healthy outdoor life.)

Must be able to multi-task. (It will be necessary to both climb and shout at the same time. And it will also be necessary to be able to hold several conversations at the same time. This child is half northern Irish, and these are mere survival skills.)

Must do 'coy' really well. (It will lead to Mum spoiling you – even though she thinks she won't. Hahahahaha!)

Must be a girl. (When her Mum was young she thought she might like a boy - just so she could play football with him. But she was wrong because, really, she wanted a girl. Point 1, above, should cover this. And Mum will know it's a girl from the minute she conceives.)

Methodology: None of the above will really matter, as she will love this child without question. And she will know that you are a blessing.

Thanks,
Grandma

P.S. Make it fun – she'll love the ride.

> In this letter I want to share the thoughts, the feelings.

So far Grandma and God are working to brief – a wonderful set of designs! I'm also pretty sure she gives you pokes every now and again, just for the kicks. I would!

So, my Heidi . . . in this letter I want to share the thoughts, the feelings - the culmination of my experiences that brought me my blessing – and why even what, at the time was the 'not so good stuff', was actually my blessing too.

> The thing with blessings is that
> they are not always obvious at first.

You see, the thing with blessings is that they are not always obvious at first. Sometimes your memories (and the beliefs you extrapolate from them) can be a type of prison sentence - but one that you can end. I mean, how can anyone actually think that the loss of your Grandma in this world could have its blessings? I mean, that just is not what we are told to think.

> I'm actually saying that you can always be in charge.

I'm not saying that this is a 'silver cloud' type situation. I'm actually saying that you can always be in charge and you can learn to connect, to evolve, to work through your emotions in your darkest days. And from them you can grow into something much better - an even better version of you but FOR you!

So . . . when your Grandma left this world (well, this dimension), it set the beginning for this wonderful transition to happen. A transition that I could never quite see in my path.

A blockage that was a gift in itself
(and which I now recognise as FEAR)

There was this great big fat blockage – a blockage that was a gift in itself (and which I now recognise as FEAR) which ultimately led me to you. And not just at the time that your dad and I were ready - but that you were ready too! You see, it was the day after Grandma's funeral that my whole world began to change. Your Grandma was/IS a wonderful woman, but I didn't always see it. And if the truth be known, I didn't feel she saw it in me for many years either. I now know this not to be true. This was my version of things, that I created in my mind. And I believed it for so long that it became my identity.

I recalled 'FEAR of God' and not the LOVE of God.

Your Grandma was an amazing woman, the kindest, most loving person. She was a deeply religious woman, of the Christian denomination. Her faith saw her through to her grave, but I just didn't connect with some of the practice. It was a very reverent version. I recalled 'FEAR of God' and not the LOVE of God. I knew and felt that LOVE was what really mattered, but I was just a kid; and I needed to go and explore the big bad world so that I could find out what my version actually was. And that led me from Northern Ireland to England, which doesn't sound very far but to my family it was kind of a big deal. It's now 22 years since I made that move.

> The one thing I thought I knew about Grandma was that somehow our belief systems were connected.

This is important: The one thing I thought I knew about Grandma was that somehow our belief systems were connected. And that the connection was a spiritual one. A LOVING one.

One day, as I was driving through the glorious mountains at home, it suddenly dawned on me that my Mum (your Grandma) was now the sky, the clouds, and the awe-inspiring mountains. I realised that she was connected to my past, present, and future - that she now totally 'got me' and that I now got her. Her spirit now transcended time and space, and it transcended her earthly body. And guess what! So does mine and yours! We are actually super beings. How inconceivably awesome is that? And for that reason Mum/Grandma hasn't gone anywhere. She is always with me, as we are all just connected to life source. We are made from the stardust!

Can you believe that!
I had no idea what I was walking into.

But this was just the beginning of the epiphany. . . .This was when I knew I really had some work to do! This was when my dear friend began drawing me to her. She knew something I didn't. (I know! Can you believe that!) She wanted to help, and I had no idea what I was walking into. I had no idea what I was going to do, so I had no preconceptions. I just walked right on in and went with the ride. You see, an epiphany is one thing, but really, this was just the beginning of the next stage of my journey - the beginning of the next transition. I had all these memories, all these beliefs, and some scars that were my burden. (We all do.)

I needed to begin to grieve.
I was running - running from my own silly fears.

I needed to begin to offload. I needed to begin to grieve, and I needed to be able to celebrate again. For I had now laden myself with thoughts and behaviours that just did not serve me anymore! I was running - running from my own silly fears - when what I actually needed to do was stare them right in the face and show them exactly who is boss!

> I was doing it to me!

I had worked too hard. I had let the life of people I cared about infect mine, and I had let people tear me down. What's worse - they weren't even trying to do it! I was doing it to me! I hid, hid behind the fun, party girl. And I was brilliant at it. By the way, I am still fun. It's just even more fun now!

> 'Tapping.' I will show this to you one day.
>
> Who knew that it's possible to unlock years and layered beliefs with a few taps on the body?

I went to see my friend, Lizzie, who does this cool thing called 'tapping.' I will show this to you one day. Its proper name is FasterEFT. Who knew that it's possible to unlock years and layered beliefs with a few taps on the body?_Okay - there is a little more to it than that - or there was for me anyway. But back then my focus was the need to grieve. I just couldn't cry it out. I needed to release . . . and memory by memory, belief by belief, my friend guided me to remove the barriers and just let me flow again.

> The releases came faster.

The tears came, and tears are actually a good thing. They are a release –

don't let anyone make you feel any different about tears! But the laughter came too with each tear, and with each belly-laugh the releases came faster and faster. I was becoming free, and that's why, I guess, they call it FasterEFT! Clever, eh!

I could not quite find the way to flick the switch.

Anyway getting back to you, my wonderful baba (that's you)! The biggest block I had of all was around having children. Your dad and I, we have an awesome relationship. But for some reason that we didn't quite fully understand, we were actually scared of having kids. I was worried I wouldn't be any good at it. I felt like I was working on it, but somehow I could not quite find the way to flick the switch. I was waiting on another epiphany - a sign - but it just doesn't always quite work like that.

Then one day, your dad and I were perusing through the garden centre. And your Grandma floated down a little white feather. It danced across me and rested on a rose bush - the rose bush that is now in the 'National Trust' pot in the yard. Your Grandma had sent me a sign, and that, my little 'HeidiKins,' was the beginning of your journey into this world and the beginning of our bond. Together, we grew! Physically and spiritually you and I connected.

You kept trying to tell me 'Mum, I'm fine!'

My bump was massive, even though you were a normal size. But you had a swimming pool to hang out in, so that was fun. You were my little turtle. We talked in our meditations. You bobbed around with me when I swam, and you gave me a nudge or two just to let me know you were okay. But I still worried, for worrying had become my nature. So I tapped on that worry (now also with Aunty Deirdre) and you kept trying to tell me 'Mum, I'm fine!'

I give thanks everyday for you
and the lessons that I've learned.

You were more than fine - you were perfect. You are perfect. Perfect as you are. Perfect each day, just as you find yourself. Where you are now is perfectly where you are meant to be. It's the perfect opportunity for you to become as perfect as you want to be. So grab it with both little hands, feel it, learn to love it, ride with it, and know that you will always be perfectly fine – just as I am too. I give thanks everyday for you and the lessons that I've learned. My life is abundant and full of love. I hope you can make yours abundant and full of love too.

Love you always,
Mum
XOXOXOXOX

Arlene lives in England with her husband and new baby daughter. She attributes many of her life-changing insights to FasterEFT and also the meditation work she has done. She credits Deirdre Maguire with influencing many of her positive changes.

This letter represents the freedom of expression that Arlene has now, especially the beauty of being able to talk to her own daughter. As Arlene has unlocked her own freedom through various modalities, ultimately she hopes to help her daughter unlock her freedom when she is older and the time is right.

Oh, What a Beautiful Mornin'

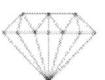

Carol Langdon

Immediately before finding Faster EFT, I was in a state of turmoil. Within the previous 6 to 8 months I had decided to leave my marriage of 28 years and had moved out. I'd recently given up my job of 14 years running slimming groups, which also integrated my formal psychology training into the problem of what makes people want to eat. Running those groups was, for me, an enormous gift throughout that period in my life, as it gave me all sorts of insights into how the mind works and how people think. I then became a volunteer driver taking cancer patients to hospital for treatment. During this time my youngest sister was trying various chemotherapy-type treatments for her melanoma (skin cancer).

I was excellent at accumulating debt!

Money was tight at that time, as it had been all of my life. The more money I tried to earn, the less I was able to earn. I had never been taught how to manage money (and neither had my parents); so this was something which did not come easily to me. In fact, I was excellent at accumulating debt!

> 'I'm not good enough! I'll never earn enough to live,'

Although I had now 'found myself' again after years of struggle, I knew that I still had a lot of work to do. I spent a lot of time researching and looking for something which would help my sister, and that at the same time could be a useful modality in my own counselling practice. I knew that I wanted to help people to deal with their problems, but the thought of seeing someone week after week, possibly for years, did not inspire me. In fact, I was feeling very resistant to doing so. I was also feeling that nobody would want to come to see me anyway. 'I'm not good enough! I'll never earn enough to live,' I thought.

Over the years I'd read lots of books on co-dependency, spirituality, the law of attraction, how to heal myself, and the list goes on. People always seemed to open up and tell me their problems - even upon first meeting them - so studying counselling was a natural progression. I was still working through the childhood sexual trauma I had experienced, but now thanks to the counselling course and training I was able to talk about it much more easily. I was even learning to sit *with* myself and accept who I was – which, quite honestly, being over 50 was very difficult! In the past I had always needed to be occupied, on the phone, out doing something, or distracted in some way almost all of the time.

> How could something this ridiculous work?
> I totally rejected it.

All that I had done so far was helpful up to a point, but surely there had to be something which helped quicker and deeper in a more healing and satisfying way! A friend of mine who had also done the same counselling course had been trying to get me interested in FasterEFT going on for a year and had been extolling its virtues to me. I had asked her what exactly it was. She said, 'You do THIS,' and showed me the tapping points. Well it seemed absolutely crazy! How could something this ridiculous work? I totally rejected it. I just didn't listen to anything she said about it and thought it was madness!

One particular morning I had a phone call from my mum telling me that my sister who was suffering from melanoma had just been told there was nothing more that could be done for her. She was now classed as terminal and was given approximately one year to live. I was devastated. My friend who used FasterEFT arrived for coffee, and I told her my news. She suggested we watch a video Robert Smith had just put up on YouTube, and we tapped along with it. I agreed because I thought this would be the only way to prove to her it doesn't work, and then perhaps she would say no more about it and leave me alone! I expected it NOT to work. It was too weird.

> My clients could be empowered to
> take control for themselves.

WOW!!! After about 10 minutes, I was proved wrong. This was what I had been looking for - for so long! After just one video, the way I saw what was happening with my sister completely changed. I realised that I had already written her off as dead in my mind and that I was wasting so much time. I also realised that by using this tool, my clients could be empowered to take control for themselves. This was something I had to learn.

I ordered my home study kit and completed Level 1 straight away because there was a live training in Belfast called 'Heal Your Sexual Self' within 6 weeks, and I decided I had to be there and do that training! While in Belfast I invested in a crossfire session with FasterEFT practitioners Beth and Deirdre for myself. I'm not exaggerating when I say that straight after I felt so much lighter. I went into that room with a severe intolerance to milk and dairy products, which I'd had for most of my life. Just before leaving the room I was able to drink milk for the first time, and it tasted sweet and creamy instead of resembling what I would imagine cow poo to taste like!

By the morning I awoke with no 'mind chatter' going on - another first in my life. No worrying about anything that wasn't happening right then. Freedom. I heard the birds singing, saw the sunshine, experienced the glorious weather, and life looked so good! Two songs came into my head: 'Oh What a Beautiful Mornin'' and "Cause I'm Happy.' They summed up my experience so well.

> Two months later her tumours had shrunk by half;
> and then by another two months on,
> the tumours on her lungs and other organs had gone.

Change after change continued to happen as I worked on myself. Life improved drastically. I went home and asked my sister if I could use her to practice on. Like me, she had been dismissive in the past. She agreed and at the same time started a trial drug. Two months later her tumours had shrunk by half; and then by another two months on, the tumours on her lungs and other organs had gone.

I asked patients I was taking to hospital if they would like to learn this technique to help them with their pain, and those that wanted to know, I taught them to tap driving along in the car! One lady was told the week before Christmas that she was being taken off treatment as there was nothing more they could do for her. She told me she just wanted to be able to see the birth of her grandchild. I taught her to tap to get a good night's sleep and cope with life.

Two weeks after the New Year she was in her wheelchair coming out of the hospital as I was going in. Her face beamed as she saw me. She told me that her friend had had to wake her that morning for her appointment because she slept so well. She was also being put back onto treatment as her tumours had started to shrink. The only thing she had been doing was tapping!!!

It has been about two years now since I found this wonderful modality. I have travelled extensively and made lots of wonderful friends. Clients are empowered and learn this process so that they may take control for themselves. My finances, while not having changed substantially, I now view in a totally different way, and I have been able to do so much more as a result. I have learned to respond to life rather than react to it. Now I notice my thoughts and question them before making rash statements or decisions.

Awareness for me has become something integral in my life. Things and people don't bother me. I can't change others, only myself. Knowledge of myself and continual healing are paramount to me now. I don't sweat the small stuff, so my life and that of my loved ones is so much better and calmer. This has saved me on so many levels, and I am grateful for everything and everyone in my life. Cures are never guaranteed, but this process enables relaxation and reduces stress in life. Who wouldn't want that for themselves and others they care about?

Carol lives in Bridgwater, Somerset, UK, and she is both a mother and grandmother. Because of her dedication to healing herself and her desire to help others, her life has been transformed over the last 7 years beyond even her own recognition. Every aspect of it has changed.

A trained counsellor, Carol believes FasterEFT was the missing tool from her virtual toolbox. She had been looking for something which would take people through the healing process more deeply and quickly when she found FasterEFT through a friend's referral.

Carol has used FasterEFT successfully with clients all around the world who have had problems ranging from stress, anxiety, depression, fears and phobias, to sexual trauma, PTSD, relationships, grief and loss, weight loss, and pain.

Carol believes the reason for her success is that she has continued to work on herself to transform her life, therefore putting her in a much better place to facilitate healing in others.

Website:
www.bridgetoreality.com

What's Wrong with Me?

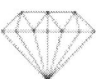

Chantal Quesnel

For God has not given us a spirit of fear, but of power and of love and of a sound mind. 2 Timothy 1:7

I grew up the older of two daughters in a family of modest means. For so many years, all I ever really wanted was to be good at something. I wanted to feel like there was something - anything - that I could say was my purpose in this lifetime and enable me to feel like I was earning my right to be here.

'What's wrong with me? Why don't people like me? Why aren't I like the other kids?'.

From a young age, I often had to manage difficult emotions. I recall feeling anxiety daily as I walked to school. I seemed to have a veritable knack for annoying people . . . other kids, teachers, or anyone. As young as age 7 or 8, I often questioned 'What's wrong with me? Why don't people like me? Why aren't I like the other kids?' This ingrained pattern of thought followed me throughout my school years. My saving grace was that I was good at singing and acting. As I auditioned for plays in high school and others noticed my talents, I realized I had found my niche. Finally I had something I could do well and say I was proud of.

> Those panic attacks were like
> tidal waves of absolute and total terror.

Wanting to pursue singing as a career, I auditioned for the voice performance program at McGill University and was accepted. I began working toward a Bachelor of Music and had set my sights on becoming an opera singer, but performance anxiety was becoming an excruciating problem as my throat would often close up just before a recital or vocal exam. I could sing easily and effortlessly one week, and then the next week I'd lose my voice completely for no apparent reason. Eventually, panic attacks started, and I went to the university health clinic. I vaguely recall seeing a psychiatrist for about a half dozen sessions without much relief. Those panic attacks were like tidal waves of absolute and total terror. And I knew the panic I felt was not just about losing my voice, but about losing what I'd built my self-esteem on. The panic was also about losing the 'me' I was becoming.

> My own body was against me.

The nerves and panic were even manifesting in various physical reactions, from my throat constricting, to sweats, shakes, and heart palpitations. I even had severe migraines, with one hellish episode resulting in hospitalization with severe dehydration from vomiting profusely. The muscular tension on the right side of my face was so severe I was literally blind in one eye causing me to miss a final exam. I recall feeling a deep sense of betrayal, like my own body was against me somehow.

The only thing we can control is our own inner perceptions, beliefs, and emotions.

I realized that if my voice was not dependable, then as a singer, I was not dependable. It was time for a change in direction. After graduation, I left Montreal and moved to Toronto, where I soon found an acting agent and began working as an actress and spokesmodel. Compared to singing, the demands of the modelling and acting industry seemed more under my control. But I chuckle now as I think of how naive I was. It would be years before I discovered the truth - that the only thing we can control is our own inner perceptions, beliefs, and emotions.

At age 23, however, I didn't know how to manage my emotions. I knew I was smart enough to easily memorize lines and scripts, so I reasoned that if I could just manage to stay 'model thin' I'd be rewarded with work. Not so. The 'rule of thumb' acting coaches tell their students is 'You will get rejected 20 times for every 1 time where you actually book the part.' Well I didn't want to believe that those statistics applied to me. The battle to prove myself was launched, and I achieved success, becoming a full ACTRA union member and working on many TV and film projects. But the competitive stress of auditioning and surviving financially in a precarious career wrought havoc inside me. I sought refuge in various forms of escapism. I loved running and even ran a full 26.2-mile marathon. While it was a healthy diversion in some ways, I knew I was running from the pain, literally and figuratively.

Alcohol became my trusted companion.
Thoughts of suicide prompted me to go into
12-step recovery.

It was around my late twenties and early thirties that I noticed I was drinking more alcohol. What started out as a glass or two of wine with dinner eventually progressed to two bottles nightly. Alcohol became my trusted companion and seemed like the perfect coping method. But while alcohol numbed the anxiety and pain at night, it brought regret, self-loathing, and remorse the next morning. I'd drink heavily, pass out, and then wake up 4 hours later unable to sleep because of withdrawal jitters. This pattern continued for 8 horrible years before thoughts of suicide prompted me to go into 12-step recovery through Alcoholics Anonymous (AA).

The panic and anxiety I felt daily
left me baffled and frustrated.

Once in AA, I did all the things I was told to do: I joined a home group, got a sponsor, went to 90 meetings in 90 days, got active in my group, and did regular service work. There is good stuff in 12-step recovery. It really did save my life and was what I needed at that time. But while I did get physically sober, AA didn't solve the years of hurts that continued to drive the constant anxiety I felt. I was still experiencing emotions of fear, anxiety, and daily panic attacks and couldn't understand what was wrong with me.

Here I was sober for years, going to meetings regularly, being sponsored, and actively sponsoring other women with a dependence on alcohol. I'd been to big book studies, 12-step retreats, and I had even become a practitioner in an energy modality. I was using it on myself, people I sponsored in AA, and I even had some regular clients. Yet the panic and anxiety I felt daily left me baffled and frustrated.

---

40 years of internal 'references and resources' were still deeply rooted inside.

Again, I tried to run from my painful emotions. I've always felt good helping others, so in an effort to escape my own inner turmoil, I threw myself into sessions with clients and AA service work. It seemed to me like a 'win-win.' The irony, however, was that as I was helping clients to cope with their anxieties, afterward I would return home and all those feelings I'd been avoiding by distracting myself would return with a vengeance. I was unaware that 40 years of internal 'references and resources' were still deeply rooted inside my subconscious mind, and it was those feelings that tormented me daily.

One day, while I was online, researching modalities that might help with addictions, I stumbled upon a YouTube video of Robert G Smith using the FasterEFT addiction protocol at the Habilitat treatment centre in Hawaii. A gentleman named Jeff Nash introduced the demonstration and spoke about FasterEFT as an alternative method that is 'a sort of hybrid of hypnosis, acupressure meridian tapping, and neurolinguistic programming.' Huh? It caught my attention. I'd heard of NLP. Years earlier I'd ordered Anthony Robbins Personal Power 30-day program on cassette tapes. So I watched Robert's talk on how the mind works and how we come into this world and form our emotional 'model' of it based on our past experiences. He talked about how our memories and imprints are the subconscious drivers that form this model. I watched more videos and tapped along on myself, 'borrowing benefits' from each person sitting in the 'magic chair' as Robert demonstrated the technique.

The releasing of so much pain was profound and lasting.

I watched Robert tap out years of deeply held beliefs on person after person. In particular, I watched and re-watched video 433, entitled 'I was feeling abandoned until today. . . . ' Each time I watched, I was substituting one after another of my own memories, and, I swear, I must have cried along with that precious red-haired lady for hours! The releasing of so much pain was profound and lasting. FasterEFT was providing the missing link I had wanted and searched for.

Wanting to learn more about FasterEFT, I ordered the Ultimate Download Collection and watched the Habilitat sessions with Wixie, Alvin, and Cameron first. I then decided to order the Track B, Ultimate Training Kit and spent a year studying the videos, tapping with other practitioners-in-training. I achieved my Level 3 FasterEFT practitioner certification through this home-study kit.

Ironically, the biggest changes I've experienced in FasterEFT have been the most subtle in terms of my perception. At one time, my self-esteem was indelibly linked to achieving financial success as an actress. I no longer hold that belief. I am enough as I live and breathe and grow and share it all. I can admit that my healing journey has been at times a slow and often tedious process. I tap on myself daily.

I have always felt proud of my father. He had only a grade 9 education, but worked hard to make something of himself, earning a modest income, first as an auto mechanic and later as a millwright. A year ago, my father was diagnosed with pancreatic cancer. He required Whipple surgery (a pancreatoduodenectomy), which is a complex and difficult procedure. I was able to tap on him to help him with his pre-surgery jitters, and he went into the hospital with a calm and positive attitude.

Despite complications and 14 hours in the operating room, he survived the surgery. I was able to be by his bedside in the intensive care unit, tapping on myself constantly as he was sleeping. When he awoke, I held his hand and in a gentle quiet voice helped him to 're-anchor' the happy memories from our pre-surgery tapping session. He had no idea what I was doing, of course; but as he was expressing how uncomfortable he was feeling I just gently brushed my fingertips on his forehead, side of his eye, under his eye, and collarbone and whispered, 'Just breath into it, and as you breath out, let it go.' And he did! He went along with it, and his early recovery progressed remarkably well.

At the time of this writing, I'm in the process of packing up and moving from Toronto to be closer to the small city where my father lives. I am beyond grateful for the time I've shared with him. A year ago, he was a robust 5' 10" and 175 pounds. Post-surgery, he's now 120 pounds and in palliative care. The cancer has metastasized to his liver. I'm just tapping and taking things one day at a time.

In earlier times, I never would have dreamed I'd leave Toronto, a city I've lived in, worked in, and auditioned in for 25 years to live in a small town. But that is exactly what I'm doing, and I will be working as a wellness coach and FasterEFT practitioner. It's exactly where I know I'm supposed to be.

> My own authentic self lies within my heart,
> and that is finally enough for me.

I no longer need to 'become' something so that I can feel worthwhile. My own authentic self lies within my heart, and that is finally enough for me. But feeling comfortable in this way has required enormous trust in myself. Robert Smith says, 'Every person who enters into your life, every situation you encounter, will leave you good gifts and bad gifts. It's up to you which gifts you choose to open and to keep.' I would be remiss if I didn't acknowledge that AA did give me gifts, my other modalities gave me gifts, and my 25 years in the film and television industry gave me gifts - and for all these gifts I am truly grateful. These experiences were all part of the circuitous path I had to take in order to find FasterEFT. And in finding FasterEFT, I've found so much truth - truth about my mind, my perceptions, my beliefs, and that my capabilities are as infinite as my beliefs allow.

This past July I had the privilege of working with Robert's amazing team of practitioners at the Habilitat Drug and Alcohol Recovery Treatment Centre in Hawaii. It was there during the Habilitat Healing Marathon that I met Level 5 master practitioner Deirdre Maguire for the first time.

I was both nervous and excited to meet the woman I'd been watching for years on YouTube and whose skill I'd admired so much. Her vivid and smiling blue eyes immediately welcomed me, and I knew there was something about her heart that I identified with. Beyond her skill and expertise, there is a dedication in Deirdre to her innermost self. Her absolute and complete willingness to share with me her experience and knowledge of FasterEFT was gracious and generous beyond words. I learned so much from observing her during the 'crossfire' sessions we did with the residents.

It taught me the power of the mind to make peace within and to heal the heart.

My experience at Habilitat was profoundly impactful. It further instilled in me the power and effectiveness of FasterEFT. It taught me the power of the mind to make peace within and to heal the heart. Working one-on-one with the men and women at Habilitat has enriched and empowered me in ways I couldn't have discovered if I hadn't gone through my past challenges.

I will close my story with my favourite two-word prayer: Thank you!

Each time I share this amazing tool, I get back that same healing exponentially. To watch someone transform and change before my eyes in a single session fills my heart with so much joy. That, to me, is true wealth of spirit. I am so blessed to have FasterEFT, and I will close my story with my favourite two-word prayer: Thank you!

Chantal Quesnel is a certified health and wellness coach and a Level 4 FasterEFT practitioner. She is a graduate of McGill University and has more than 20 years of experience as an actress, professional keynote speaker, television host, and voiceover artist. She has voiced more than 100 television and radio commercials and station promotions for Canadian media. An avid marathon runner, she also hosted two seasons of CTV Sportsnet's THE RUNNING ZONE.

To address her own debilitating anxiety, depression, and severe panic attacks, Chantal trained as a practitioner in several healing methodologies. She continues to pursue her interest in epigenetics, psychoneuroimmunology, neuro-linguistic programming, hypnosis, and other modalities.

Chantal works with clients internationally via Skype and phone, as well as in person.

Email:

chantalquesnel1@gmail.com

Website:

http://fasterett.com/talk-to-a-practitioner/?user_id=37866

I Didn't Have Huge Traumas

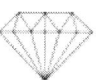

Deirdre Brocklebank

I attended my first FasterEFT (Faster Emotionally Focused Transformations) workshop with Robert Smith (the creator of FasterEFT) in Melbourne, Australia in 2010. At the workshop, I listened to and acknowledged others' stories of why they came to learn about and to study FasterEFT. As I attended many of Robert's later workshops, I heard how FasterEFT has changed many of the participants' lives.

I didn't think I needed healing for myself.
I didn't have the huge traumas.

I didn't think I needed healing for myself. Therefore, I initially felt a bit 'out of it,' as I didn't have the huge traumas and then the shifts that others appeared to experience from tapping with FasterEFT. I thought I was only going to the workshops because I wanted to learn more. My intention was to be able to help others more effectively with their issues. It was to be an adjunct to reflexology, pranic healing, Reiki, and other modalities that I used.

Looking back, I believed that my life was very good and I had it all together. That was, until Robert helped me to release deep-seated emotions I had been holding around my mother's death. As I continued to use FasterEFT for myself and with the help of others, the layers continued to peel off. I realised just how much I was still being run by my many programs. For example, I was still that little girl seeking approval, still dealing with issues of abandonment (including being sent to boarding school) and still healing around my brother's many serious illnesses and traumatic incidents which impacted on the entire family.

My son was critically ill with meningitis when he was very young. This left him with a severe hearing loss. FasterEFT helped me to let go of my pain, guilt, fear, sadness, anger, recriminations, etc, that I felt because of his illness and suffering. But above all, it gave me the opportunity to identify with how my mother would have felt when she was nursing my brother through his many illnesses. Consequently, I was able to acknowledge, thank, and love her for her gifts to me of resilience, love, compassion, and tolerance that gave me the strength to support my son – and to adapt to his significantly altered life.

FasterEFT also helped me to heal issues with my father. I felt that he had not been there for me for most of my life. After addressing my feelings of hurt, rejection, abandonment, etc, around this issue with tapping, I was able to see life from his perspective and to feel love and gratitude for him. I could now understand that, even though he was assessed as having manic depression, he was a sensitive, highly intelligent, and gifted man. I realised that he has passed on many gifts to me, including the thirst for knowledge which lead me to FasterEFT.

Through FasterEFT I have forged strong, new friendships; and I feel part of a very professional community which has supported me, both professionally and privately. I am very grateful to my colleagues who were there on Skype, or in person, to assist me to address an issue or a memory that was troubling me.

I have also had the opportunity to travel to other places for workshops in Australia to meet and to share with like-minded people. One of the highlights of my journey with FasterEFT was being invited by Robert to work with residents at Habilitat – an alcohol and drug rehabilitation centre in Hawaii. It was there that I truly learned about the resilience of human nature and received further confirmation that we can heal ourselves of even the most seemingly hopeless and painful life situations, once we let go of the past and take control of our lives.

There are no broken people,

just people operating from hurt and broken ideas.

Thanks to Robert I learned that, 'there are no broken people, just people operating from hurt and broken ideas.' This is one of the most profound teachings of FasterEFT for me. It is also a revelation to my own clients when I tell them this, particularly those who have been living under the label of 'depression' or any other medical term. I feel very privileged to witness their self-realisation that they are doing it themselves and that there is nothing 'wrong' with them. FasterEFT teaches that they can change whatever it is that they are holding inside so they can have the life that they want.

For me, one of the biggest bonuses from learning FasterEFT is that I have been able to teach my grandchildren this tapping skill that they can use for the rest of their lives. The result of this has been my book, _Suraya's Secret For You: How you can change from unhappy to happy_, through which I hope to reach out to other children. In the book, my granddaughter Suraya shares how she has used FasterEFT tapping to help herself to let go of many things that were troubling her. By using this tapping technique, I believe that Suraya - as well as my other grandchildren and any other children who are taught the skill - will literally have the world at their fingertips. I am so grateful to be able to leave this legacy for my grandchildren and their future children.

I believe that I have achieved my original goal to be able to help my clients even more by including FasterEFT with my other modality skills. This belief is supported by my case notes and many testimonials that I have received from grateful clients.

The following examples are a rewarding and positive confirmation for me of the amazing effectiveness of FasterEFT.

What does feeling abandoned and not loved have to do with an injured knee?
I had a client who had knee surgery a few weeks before I saw her. She hobbled in on a walking frame and, with great difficulty, managed to get down three steps to my clinic. We addressed whatever came up in her memories. These included feelings of abandonment, not feeling loved, etc, when she was sent away to boarding school, along with other issues regarding nuns and relationships.

When we finished the session she was able to walk without her stick and with only a slight stiffness in the knee that had been operated on. She was also able to walk more easily back up the three steps without her stick. This was in sharp contrast to how difficult it had been for her to negotiate the steps when she first arrived.

The next session she used her stick for support, but her knee was much stronger. In essence, I had just followed her lead and her memories and feelings by asking, 'How do you know?,' which is a statement used in FasterEFT to help the client focus on feelings, beliefs, and memories that produce symptoms.

Grieving

My friend had high blood pressure, and he was very red faced and anxious. He was suffering while thinking about his daughter, who had died 18 months previously. She hadn't wanted him to see her so ill, so she asked him not to go to her. His friends had tried to encourage him to go despite what she had said. However, he decided not to, and he was now feeling terrible about that. I tapped and 'spoke for him' for a few minutes, as he felt too emotional to speak. His skin colour changed to a more normal hue, and he said he no longer felt bad. He had no previous experience of FasterEFT, and he was much relieved to experience such a huge, significant change in the way he felt in such a short time.

> A person doesn't have to believe in FasterEFT
> for it to produce significant changes for them.

'No-content' tapping - The sceptic

This case demonstrates that a person doesn't have to believe in FasterEFT for it to produce significant changes for them.

When I visited my friend in hospital she was in a lot of pain and fearful of breathing, as it really hurt her. Her chest had been badly bruised when she was resuscitated prior to being admitted to the emergency unit the previous night. She allowed me to tap on her, although she didn't understand what I was doing.

She didn't tell me until days later that before I first tapped on her, she had been feeling very frightened. This was because when she was admitted to hospital, she was bleeding from her bowel. As her five sisters had died from cancer (some of them from bowel cancer), she thought that she might also have cancer.

I don't understand or believe in what you are doing. However, I always feel better after it, so whatever you do seems to be working.

My friend emailed me soon after she was released from hospital, to thank me - yet expressing her lack of belief in tapping. She said: 'I'm amazed that the tapping helped me as I'm a bit of a sceptic, but I'm very grateful. I don't understand or believe in what you are doing. However, I always feel better after it, so whatever you do seems to be working.'

Four years later, she now tells me and others that I saved her life. She also told me that her daughter thought the change in her mother was a 'miracle' and that she couldn't believe how much healthier and more relaxed she looked after I tapped on her.

'No content' tapping – Professionally challenging

This is a quote from a client who is an accredited counsellor and psychotherapist:

Sorry for my delay in responding, I wanted to see if it lasted. FasterEFT was such a challenge to my own training and therapeutic background. I had had that traumatic memory since childhood and despite years of therapy it still caused me distress. I couldn't believe that such a short session could deal with the pain. Four months later it's still gone.

I still don't know the issues I tapped on with this client, but our session of just 10 to 15 minutes resulted in a significant change.

'Abreaction' - I thought I had dealt with that!

During the information gathering with a new client, he said that he was sent to boarding school when he was eight. He told me that he didn't have any feelings about it, as he'd had counselling for it. He didn't show any reaction at all while talking about it. I decided to ask him about it anyway because he had raised the issue. I asked him what his name was when he went to boarding school. It was a longer version of what he is now called. I started tapping on him using the name he had as a child. Almost immediately he had an incredibly strong, emotional abreaction. He leaned forward with his chest on his legs and his hands on either side of his face. He then started rocking, sobbing, and crying loudly. This lasted a couple of minutes.

When he recovered, he was stunned at the intensity of his reaction, as he had told me that he doesn't normally show emotion and he thought he 'had dealt with it with counselling.'

It was a valuable lesson for me to explore an issue and/or memory when it is raised and not assume that there is no emotional intensity, just because my client tells me so.

> He was amazed that FasterEFT helped him to
> let go of this fear so quickly.

Fear/terror of rats and mice

My client had had a fear and sometimes terror of rats and mice for over 39 years. After 'flipping' his memories, I showed him photos of swarms of rats and mice. He couldn't believe that he now saw them as 'cute and just rats and mice.' He also now saw their eyes as friendly. This was a huge change from his description of them in his original memories. He was amazed that FasterEFT helped him to let go of this fear so quickly. In fact, the change happened so fast that I had time within his hour-long appointment to also clear his back pain that he had had for as long as he could remember.

Swallowing and sweetness

I love the fact that FasterEFT can often produce results very quickly. I tend to tap on anyone, anywhere and anytime, with their permission. For example, at lunch in Melbourne one day I was talking to a woman from a workshop that we were both attending. She mentioned that she had a lump in her throat from stress and was finding it hard to swallow. I did the FasterEFT 'Quick Tap' technique, plus a few additional rounds of tapping. She was able to then swallow water without any difficulty. The most interesting feedback was that she said the water tasted sweet. This was amazing, as it was only Melbourne tap water, and she hadn't been able to taste sweetness for several months.

Addiction to diet soft drinks and caffeinated energy drinks
This client let go of her addiction to a type of diet soft drink (or fizzy drink) and other caffeinated energy drinks. She tells it in her own words:

Before working with Deirdre I was drinking at least 2-3 cans of caffeinated drinks a day. Sometimes more! These drinks were not only an expensive habit, but I also knew they were filled with chemicals that are not good for me.

I had given up these drinks in the past, without using FasterEFT and I had found the process difficult (many cravings) and I ended up with a week-long migraine. This time I got Deirdre's help and it was simple and easy. I had no withdrawal symptoms (headache free) and my cravings disappeared too! Thanks to Deirdre I'm now drinking 2-3 litres of water a day and feel healthier and I'm saving money.

Limited potential
Prior to doing the FasterEFT sessions with me, my client felt very confused about her future, both professionally and personally. However, after doing the sessions, she applied for and was offered two well-paid positions. She also resolved her relationship issues with her partner:

I really enjoyed working with Deirdre over the past 6 months and feel more like myself than ever before. I cried and laughed and I felt completed, supported and safe as I shed tears of emotional trauma that was unconsciously limiting my potential.

Depression
I have had great feedback from a client's wife. Her husband came to me in February for medically diagnosed depression. She said that he was very unhappy about his health when he first came to see me. He was feeling that nothing could help him, as he had not benefited from psychiatric help. According to his wife, 'He is now jumping out of his skin.' She now believes that, 'He is once again the man I married, with more joy in his life.' I think these are impressive results, considering he has had just two sessions of FasterEFT and one session of FasterEFT plus reflexology.

Because she saw how much FasterEFT has helped her husband, the woman has now become my client and has just had her first session with me for her medically diagnosed depression!

Manifesting money with FasterEFT
Money was always a big issue with me, as I was raised in a family where we were frequently told, 'Money doesn't grow on trees' and 'You have to work hard to earn money.' Tapping has helped me to clear many of my programs around these beliefs.

Manifesting money with tapping has become fun and effective for me. For example, I tapped on the 'KC' or 'karate chop' point of hand while stating,

'I always have more than enough of everything.' While tapping on the 'CB' or collar bone, I tapped and affirmed, 'I am willing and able to share what I have with others with love.'

Some of the benefits that I obtained from tapping on those points with the affirmations were: more new clients; a large order for some charts that I created; an unexpected cheque from my essential oils supplier (when it is usually very much the other way around); and a 'windfall' payment of interest from a credit union account I hadn't used for years and had cancelled.

FasterEFT also enabled me to resolve relationship issues which were somehow connected to my attitude towards money and abundance generally. As a result, I feel more abundant in all things, and money always flows when and where required.

Self-help swimming

It's great that I can not only use FasterEFT to help others, but I can also apply it quickly and creatively for my own issues without getting bound up with theory and protocols. For example, I was swimming laps recently. I hadn't swum any distance for a few months, so I found it a bit of an effort. I started to feel very nauseous. I was considering stopping swimming - but instead, I decided to tap. I visualised each point, and as I moved through them I mentally repeated 'let it go' with each swimming stroke.

After about a length (just over a minute), I no longer felt sick. I was able to finish my laps and complete my swim. Without the tapping I would have had to stop swimming, as I was very close to being sick in the water.

Long term breast pain

My experience supports what Robert says: that pain is about relationships and, secondly, that persistence pays. For years I had been experiencing intermittent pain and tissue tension in my left breast. The numerous medical examinations, ultrasounds, and infrared imaging showed there was no physical reason for the pain, tension, and discomfort.

FasterEFT helped, but it didn't immediately resolve the emotional causes until after the intensive sessions that I did this year. Thanks to the combined skills of some of my colleagues, I no longer have pain. The tension has gone, the tissue feels normal, and the ultrasound didn't show anything of concern.

I am continuing on my journey in my quest to help myself and others to realise our full potential and to achieve the life that we want while having F.U.N. (my acronym for Freeing Unwanted Negativity), along the way. I offer my profound thanks to Robert G Smith in particular and to all others who have helped me along my path!

Deirdre Brocklebank is an experienced FasterEFT, Level 4 advanced practitioner, an NLP practitioner, and a certified reflexologist. She is also the author of a children's book: SURAYA'S SECRET FOR YOU: HOW YOU CAN CHANGE FROM UNHAPPY TO HAPPY, which teaches children how to use FasterEFT to address their problems.

Over the last 20 years, Deirdre has incorporated many techniques into her work from her home-based clinic in Canberra, Australia, but she now focuses mainly on FasterEFT and reflexology.

Deirdre specialises in anxiety, stress, and addictions. Her aim is to help people of all ages to live happier, healthier lives. Over the years her clients have responded positively to her sessions addressing many physical and/or emotional conditions. These include muscular/skeletal pain, asthma, and allergies – as well as emotional states, such as post-natal depression, general depression, fears, phobias, addictions, PTSD, grief, loss, trauma, relationship issues, feeling stuck, and overwhelm.

Deirdre has written numerous articles on the use of modalities to improve health, many of which have been published in magazines, newsletters, and on the web.

For more information, including case study outcomes plus testimonials from clients, visit her website.

Deirdre provides sessions via Skype as well as in-person.

Website:

www.fastereftoz.com.au.

Skype:

skypebrock21

Link to Deirdre's Children's Book:

http://fastereftoz.com.au/surayas-secret

You're Not Dying Now

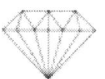

Deirdre Maguire

It's 2 a.m. I am in Hawaii. And I'm dying.

The pain comes in my body, and the voice in my mind confirms it.

Too scary to tap. Too real to tap. Too much to tap. Don't ask me to tap. YOU CAN'T ASK ME TO TAP.

Tapping's all right for emotional things but… this **is** cancer after all. It **is** real.

As I look down the barrel of my own emotional gun, my mind flashes back to conversations with another practitioner when I recall saying to her of her Fibromyalgia recovery account – "It's alright for you – You've got a story! I don't have one!"

Be careful what you ask for –you will definitely get it.

Well, be careful what you ask for – because you just might get it. I'll rephrase that.

Be careful what you ask for –you will definitely get it.

I definitely had a story now. The question was would I live to tell it?

9 months earlier and my life seemed to be finally turning the corner. I was getting what I wanted. Supporting myself by living my passion. Faster EFT Master Practitioner. Travelling the world. Having fun and helping people. At the top of my game…

The biggest NO of my life. The biggest YES to me.
Yes to my own inner wisdom.

And then - there it was – a lump in my neck – a cancer diagnosis. The medical solution for what the doctor described as an aggressive cancer in my tonsil and some lymph nodes was surgery to the neck followed by 6 weeks of radiation and chemotherapy. Long story short – I said yes to the surgery and no to the chemo and radiation. The biggest NO of my life. The biggest YES to me. Yes to my own inner wisdom.

So I said no and left Ireland for my beloved Habilitat where I knew there would be healing and support from Robert and my FasterEFT community and the residents my Habilitat* family.

But I have to say – it's one thing to say no – it's another thing to deal with the outcomes of our decisions. Say no and then take the consequences…

The fear reaches the point of no return.

So here I am. Lying in a top bunk in the female dorm in Habilitat. World famous drugs and alcohol rehabilitation unit. I'm there to volunteer my work with the residents and as a training coordinator with the newer practitioners.

12 other girls slumber while I play out the grim reality in my mind that I am in fact dying. With every sordid, terrifying aspect that accompanies not only death but a cancer death, my mind makes pictures that play havoc with my sanity. The fear reaches the point of no return.

The lowest point …

There is nothing left but to …

Tap.

The turning point…

Slowly I lift my 2 fingers to my head and I begin to tap. Repeating 'let it go' in my mind over and over as I silently tap; gradually the peak of agony in my mind subsides and there is some relief…

– And then - after an hour and a half of tapping (eternity in fear time) the thought comes – 'Well, you're not dying now, Deirdre. You're not actually dying now - In this minute – Now - Are you? …

So you might as well live. You might as well live right now. In this minute. Now. You might as well tap on the fear and live now …

And so it began.

In that moment I began to live. In that moment I believe the unconscious judge signalled to the conscious jury that it was ok to go with the verdict to live. The conscious and the unconscious making peace with each other.

In that moment, I continued to tap. And live. In the moment.

Now.

And then in the next one. **Now.**

And then the one after that. **Now.**

And slowly I got an inkling of what it's like to live now.

Now.

Not in the past. It was gone. Not in the future. I didn't have it.

But right now.

In my mind. In the dark. In that bunk. In that dorm. In that Rehab. Habilitat. Place of Change.

> Life is really all about mastering the art of gratitude
> for the miracle of just this moment…

In those moments I began to learn, not just intellectually, but (and this is the crucial key component) in the **experience** of it, that life is really all about mastering the art of gratitude for the miracle of just this moment…

> Abnormal was normal.

Living my life in a state of stress had been habitual for as long as I could remember. Not that I knew that of course. Back then, abnormal was normal.

Childhood experiences - both at home and at school - had kept me in the customary stress state of "fight-flight freeze". Compounded by the political and cultural chaos of war torn Northern Ireland, this continued into my adult life. A directionless career. A childless marriage that ended. The suicide of my father. To name but a few.

Confusion in my emotional world fuelled my destructive and sometimes reckless life. Drinking and smoking were my main coping tools – and I was very skilled at both! I worked too hard, and played too hard.

> The conscious and subconscious records (memories) I was carrying provided the "proof" for my belief that I would never be "good enough"

Despite various achievements in my life - an honours degree, partner in a family business, completing three marathons, a 200-mile maracycle, climbing Mount Kilimanjaro, and trekking in the Himalayas, my sense of self-worth was rock bottom. Why? Because the conscious and subconscious records (memories) I was carrying at that time provided the "proof" for my belief that I was a guilty disappointment and I would never be "good enough".

I first came across FasterEFT when my brother and business partner, Paul found Robert Smith's videos on YouTube.

My mum, dad, brother and myself had been running the family furniture business together. We (I am the eldest of 5 children, and my mother) were all traumatised by my father's tragic death, and Paul had the further pain of losing his mentor, friend and daily work companion.

FasterEFT had offered Paul relief for himself and his family. The changes prompted Paul to continue watching the FasterEFT videos on YouTube, and he tapped along with them.

One morning, he arrived in to work very upbeat. He had discovered that Robert Smith was to hold a seminar in Cork, Ireland. Excited and delighted that my brother had found something that worked for him, we set about organising for Paul and his family to make the trip to the other end of the country to meet Robert. I would stay behind and take care of the business.

On a phone call, a few days later, Paul and his wife, Tracey could only rave about how brilliant Robert was, and I finally decided I wanted to know more. I set about booking an appointment with this man.

I remember how foolish and nervous I felt about asking for help

---

As I took time out of my work to make the phone call I will always remember how foolish and nervous I felt about asking for help (this I remember to this day when a client calls me). As it happened, Robert was about to leave for Greece but he offered to meet me at the airport. "Not possible," I said, "I am at the other end of the country!"
He said if I paid his airfare to Greece, he would change his ticket and come to Newcastle to see me. As a million thoughts raced through my head, and as many emotions ran through my body, Robert's declaration that he could 'get rid of my demons' sealed the deal.

It was October 2009, fate stepped in, and Robert Smith was on his way to Newcastle, County Down, Northern Ireland.

can you Believe it !

In a confusion of apprehension and excitement, (we are both quite shy ☺) I welcomed Robert into my home, and invited 40 friends and family to hear him speak in my living room. Borrowing chairs from a local hotel, I was able to share this amazing man and his powerful message with those closest to me. In addition, Robert tapped on myself and family members in private sessions. He encouraged me to sit in and watch the work; I bought the Ultimate Training Home Study Kit, and thus unfolded the next stepping-stone on the journey of my life's true destination.

I spent that winter watching the DVDs, and in February 2010, I attended my first FasterEFT training seminar: Levels I and II in Oklahoma City, USA. The formidable connections and life-long friendships forged with the incredible people I met during that week were second only to the powerful passion fuelled in me to share this work and show others just like me that there is another way…

Life is always about exchange.

My FasterEFT journey led me to complete all levels of training, attaining the top certification of Master Practitioner in October 2012. Working with thousands of people, on an incredible range of challenges, the highlight of my work has been serving in Habilitat. My relationship with this unique Place of Change is a story in itself for another day. To sum it up for now let me just say: Life is always about exchange.

Up until that time I had certainly seen and experienced changes with FasterEFT. As a Master Practitioner I had helped a lot of people, and I'd even played my integral part in helping Robert Smith take this already powerful modality to the next level.

> My real purpose was to find the gift in the crisis.
> To make the lowest point the turning point.
> FasterEFT was the system that enabled me
> to let my mind and body heal itself.

But as I teach my clients and practitioners today, my real purpose during the night of the *dance with cancer* was

To find the gift in the crisis.

To make the lowest point the turning point…

Without FasterEFT I could not have done it.

Without FasterEFT I would not have had the awareness, the understanding and most importantly, crucially, the system that enabled me to let my mind and body heal itself.

> My body knows EXACTLY how to heal.

As people who've been through the cancer experience know, whether personally or with family, once it comes into the field of vision, it just seems to take over.

"My body knows EXACTLY how to heal," I tapped and reframed every single time. Every time I felt the pangs of pain that caused the familiar rush of fear. Every time I heard another sad story. Every time I got that look from someone. "Are you in remission? Did you get the all clear?" Every time there was another death. Every time I felt the guilt when I was living and they weren't.

How I felt was determined by where I put my focus.

Through FasterEFT, and everything else I had learned about the mind-body connection, I knew that the most important factor in healing and staying healthy was how I felt. I also knew that how I felt was determined by where I put my focus.

FasterEFT taught me how to change them!

FasterEFT taught me, not only that where I put my focus was decided by my subconscious records, but crucially, FasterEFT taught me how to change them!

When I was diagnosed with cancer, as terrifying as it was, I was aware that my knowledge of how the mind and body work would be an essential part of my recovery. With the amazing help and support of Robert and other friends and FasterEFT practitioners, I got through the darkness, doubt and fear of perhaps the most challenging experience of my life.

All that was four years ago …

Since then, a lot of taps.

And a lot of *"nows"*…

Powerhouse of Peace Self Mastery Program*

Today I am happier and healthier than I have ever been before. I continue to use FasterEFT in conjunction with my **Powerhouse of Peace Self Mastery Program** and am living a life I love every day. The person I am today is the result of removing the subconscious programs that were hiding the real me before. I am finally thriving in the now, as my authentic self, with a passion that serves countless others to do the same.

This great adventure called life.
Moment by moment. Now.

As I write this I am celebrating my sixtieth year, and I can safely say I am childlike in the giddiness of joy, to think about what could be coming next; but above all, I am deeply grateful to get to live this great adventure called life. Moment by moment. Now.

Series of books, workshops, private sessions, and online programs, designed to encourage and empower the individual to commit, connect and create a better life

Deirdre is a World Class Mind Wellness Expert, Life Coach, Author and Master Change Agent. She facilitates transformation at the deepest level through her workshops, seminars, and private sessions by maximising her expertise in the latest cutting edge science of transformation. At the forefront of healing, Deirdre travels the world as a Speaker, Trainer, and Master Practitioner. Empowering people to finally take control, Deirdre shows them how to take charge and put themselves in the driver's seat of their lives.

Website:
www.deirdremaguire.com

YouTube:
www.youtube.com/wisdomofIreland

Facebook:
www.facebook.com/wisdomofireland

Deirdre's Book:
MY ON PURPOSE PLANNER – The Definitive Happy Journal:
https://www.amazon.co.uk/My-Purpose-Planner-Definitive-Journal/dp/1537545140

No Longer a Victim

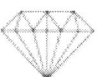

Elizabeth McPherson Thompson

Like all good tales there is a beginning. For me it was the winter of 2012 . . .

In a two-hour time span, my world was altered in ways that conventional therapy hadn't even come close to in almost 26 years.

Can you remember where you were when your life changed? Sometimes change is gradual, and sometimes it happens in an instant. That particular winter it was in an instant. And the instant occurred with Deirdre Maguire, a FasterEFT Master, and another young FasterEFT practitioner. In a two-hour time span, my world was altered in ways that conventional therapy hadn't even come close to in almost 26 years.

My history had been one of childhood sexual molestation, assault, and rapes - as well as physical and emotional pain and abuse beginning when I was about 5. Those memories and my beliefs about them and myself had been the basis of the choices I would make about my life for the next 50-plus years. That pattern lasted throughout the majority of my adult life. Oh, there had been some changes. I was no longer in abusive relationships, and

I was no longer actively suicidal. Those were two monumental changes! However, in that fateful encounter with this new modality called FasterEFT, all my fears that I was forever doomed to a life of abuse, misunderstandings, fear, rejection, and loneliness shifted. The simple phrase 'Let it go' and the skill of Deirdre Maguire helped to make that possible. Core philosophies that I didn't even know I believed were able to surface through FasterEFT. Then they were addressed in a simple, caring, and forthright manner that set the foundation for a new and better life.

It is now four years later, and, in all areas, my life has changed dramatically.

It is now four years later, and, in all areas, my life has changed dramatically. I am happily married, and I see myself as a loving, caring, functioning woman who is no longer afraid to be seen or heard. I am also now an Advanced Certified Level 4 FasterEFT Practitioner. I have made multiple trips to Las Vegas and Oklahoma City for FasterEFT training – and have even traveled to Europe, Canada, and Ireland for the same purpose. I have twice served as a volunteer at Habilitat, a premier drug and alcohol rehab centre in Hawaii.

I also volunteered with my local Rape and Abuse Center working with abused women and children - and my local prison, where I was able to teach the principles, beliefs, and basic techniques of FasterEFT to inmates as well as the officers.

> I am no longer a victim or survivor.
> And this all began with those moments during my very first FasterEFT session.

The gift Deirdre so skillfully bestowed, of actually healing parts of me that I didn't know were still hurting (and then teaching me how to proceed on my own), became the turning point of my life! I am no longer a victim or survivor. I am an empowered woman! I now have the skills to heal and change any part of my life, as well as any belief I have that keeps me bound to a past that no longer exists except in my mind. And this all began with those moments during my very first FasterEFT session.

Deirdre's determination, compassion, authenticity, and personal transformations are a blueprint for anyone looking to effectively change his or her life. Deirdre not only talks the talk. She, by example, walks the walk. I, for one, am grateful.

My Choices; My Path

In a world where instant gratification to heal is expected of every technique and modality, I wanted more. Suffice it to say, my life has taken me on many different paths, not all of which were the simplest to understand, work, or integrate into my life. Nonetheless, I knew that there was something out there that was meant to help me on this path of discovery and healing . . . and in finding it I found my passion to serve and help others.

Elizabeth McPherson Thompson is an Advanced Level 4 FasterEFT practitioner who lives in Pennsylvania, in the United States. She has studied extensively under the guidance and supervision of Robert Smith and is now providing others with the skillsets and opportunities to choose a new path in life with the goal: Educate, Inspire and Transform.

As an Emotional Fitness Coach, Elizabeth successfully uses FasterEFT to help clients change their lives. She specialises in: Domestic Violence Survivors, Sexual Assault Survivors, Anger Issues, Fears, Phobias, Addictions, Post-Traumatic Stress Disorder, Relaxation, Pain, Grief and Loss.

Elizabeth looks forward to helping you find the life you dream of. Every decision is a choice for a new beginning.

A Path of Choices

Towanda, Pennsylvania

Website:
www.apathofchoices.com

Email:
apathofchoices@gmail.com

Telephone:
(+1) 570-485-5913

The Power to Heal Was Mind the Whole Time!

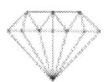

Heather Bolton McKean

They say that it's always darkest before the dawn. In my case, that was true.

If this pain continues, I want to die. I have to die.

Rock bottom for me, my darkest point, was crawling across my bedroom floor in a vain attempt to reach the bathroom. I gave up midway and just lay on the floor sobbing. The pain that I was in was unimaginable and all-consuming. I remember thinking to myself, 'If this pain continues, I want to die. I have to die.' That was in December, 2012.

Although I grew up eventually, I never grew out of it.

I was no stranger to pain or illness. As long as I could remember, I was always coming down with something. I ate antibiotics like other children ate Flintstone vitamins. It seems as if I had mumps, measles, intestinal infections, or strep throat every other month. The barrage of illness was impressive but 'normal' to me. It's all I really knew. And although I grew up eventually, I never grew out of it.

In 2000, I had a major accident that led to debilitating neck and back pain. This put me on the downward spiral of muscle relaxers, anti-inflammatories, and pain killers. At one point I was taking 6 Vicodin at a time and it barely touched the pain. The doctors did surgeries, increased my pain meds, and eventually diagnosed me with degenerative disc disease and ankylosing spondylitis. The prognosis was grim.

I was constantly fatigued and was finding it harder and harder to function.

In 2006, I was treated for infertility. I had been diagnosed with endometriosis 5 years prior and had two subsequent surgeries for that disorder. By the Grace of God, I fell pregnant one year later but had a very high risk pregnancy. Soon after my first daughter was born, I fell pregnant again. A short while later, we moved our household. All the physical and emotional stresses took their toll. By the time my second daughter was 3 months old, I couldn't even hold her without agonizing pain in my neck. I promptly received surgery to fuse the vertebrae in my spine. During this time, however, I was also feeling worse and worse in general. I was constantly fatigued and was finding it harder and harder to function. While my second child was still a baby, I was diagnosed with fibromyalgia, chronic fatigue syndrome, and rheumatoid arthritis.

can you Believe it !

I had jumped head first
down a wide and dangerous rabbit hole.

A few friends I knew during this time were battling Lyme disease and suggested I get tested. Soon, I was seeing one of the top Lyme doctors on the east coast of the United States. The diagnosis was confirmed, but to top it off, my doctor found that I had more strains of Lyme than any patient she had ever seen. I soon found myself on more and more medications, including weekly intravenous infusions. I had jumped head first down a wide and dangerous rabbit hole.

I had a cardiologist, a rheumatologist, a spine surgeon, a neurologist, an internal medicine specialist, and an infectious disease doctor on speed dial.

By December 2012, I was mostly bedridden. Laboratory results and other medical tests added parasites, malaria, heart problems, and a myriad of other diseases to my list. I had tried everything - I mean EVERYTHING - to get better. I had a cardiologist, a rheumatologist, a spine surgeon, a neurologist, an internal medicine specialist, and an infectious disease doctor on speed dial. I had tried acupuncture, acupressure, counseling, hypnosis, yoga, Traditional Chinese Medicine, Ayurvedic medicine, juice cleanses, colonics, chiropractic, energetic healing, and SO much more. Nothing seemed to help.

> I was taking 180 medications, supplements, or injections each day.

I had to be put on full disability and could barely function. I was having mini-strokes that would cause me to lose my ability to speak or focus. I was taking 180 medications, supplements, or injections each day. I had reached liver and kidney failure.

> Because I believed I had made peace with it all and had 'moved on,' I didn't think it bothered me anymore.

My life was passing me by. My children could barely touch me, and my husband was having to work AND raise the children on his own - all while trying to take care of me.

Throughout my years of illness, I had heard mention of 'tapping.' It had come up on numerous occasions, but I never looked into it. In late January of 2013, a doctor came to my house to work on my back. Knowing how much I was suffering, he suggested I explore 'tapping' modalities. Feeling desperate, I researched the topic online, and as I read about trauma being held in the body, I thought it made some sense. I had grown up in a family of addiction and abuse. Generations of trauma had been passed down. I myself had been a victim of physical, verbal, and sexual abuse. But because I believed I had made peace with it all and had 'moved on,' I didn't think it bothered me anymore.

After more Google searches, I was directed to YouTube and within minutes was watching Robert Smith use FasterEFT to help a woman stop a migraine. I honestly cannot tell you what it was that made such a strong impression on me. I hadn't even watched the entire video when I decided I HAD to try this.

I immediately contacted a FasterEFT practitioner to set up a session. At this point, my husband and I were in a very sad financial state. With me not working, and the medical bills piling up for years, we had no funds to pay for the sessions. But I was desperate. The practitioner responded to me within the day and mentioned that she didn't have any openings for 2 weeks because she was attending the FasterEFT Level 1 training soon. In a rash (but life-changing) moment, I asked if I could attend the training. She said that anyone was welcome to attend, but it was the following week in Oklahoma City.

Mommy is going to get her back fixed.

The next week, I set off for Oklahoma, barely able to lift my suitcase - over half of which was filled with the myriad of medications that I was taking. As I left, I told my little girls 'Mommy is going to get her back fixed.'

I knew that all my diseases, pain, and problems were coming from one place - my own mind.

The next day, I found myself sitting in front of Robert Smith. As I heard him speak about FasterEFT, the 'Upper and Lower models of the World' and the 'Trance Monkey' . . . I knew. I knew that all my diseases, pain, and problems were coming from one place - my own mind. A few hours later, I found myself sitting in the 'magic chair' at the front of the room as Robert's volunteer.

> What if it doesn't work? Nothing ever works.

Mostly I was terrified for Robert to use FasterEFT on me, especially in front of the entire training class. 'What if it doesn't work?' 'Nothing ever works.' "He has never worked with someone as sick as me.' 'I'm different.' But there was also a still, small voice in the background asking an even more important question: 'What if it does work?'

> The pain that was confirmed by
> X-rays and MRIs . . . gone!

It did work! In 40 minutes, the pain I had felt for so many years was gone - the pain that the doctors told me would only get worse. The pain that was confirmed by X-rays and MRIs . . . gone! I could not believe it. To test it out, I woke up the next morning and did YOGA! Gently, mind you . . . but yoga!

The rest of the week flew by! I tapped on myself constantly. I was a complete mess emotionally, but my physical pain was gone.

I went home the next week happier than I ever remember being. I had my life back! Not all of my physical symptoms disappeared in that first week. I still had LOADS of work to do! I quickly bought a package of sessions with a trained practitioner and got busy cleaning up my memories. I also tapped with other newer practitioners for practice and began working on my friends and family. Day by day I got stronger and healthier. I had follow-up appointments with all my doctors to keep track of my progress and to begin slowly weaning from my prescription medicines.

In 3 months' time, I was off of all medications!

In 3 months' time, I was off of all medications! My life had done a complete turn-around. I was happier, healthier, and finally I saw hope for my future. I attended the Level 2 training that June and really began working towards becoming the best FasterEFT practitioner I could be. I wanted others to have what I had.

It wasn't just the shift in my pain –
it was the shift in my thinking.

Many people have heard my story. I truly believe that it has helped many people have hope. But my story can also be a stumbling block for many. They want complete healing in 40 minutes, 'Just like Heather!' But the fact of the matter is that I was not 'completely healed' in that moment. It took months for some things to come right and even years for other things. BUT, I did receive the biggest shift in that first day. And it wasn't just the shift in my pain - it was the shift in my thinking. I finally took full and total responsibility for my 'problems.' I realized that if I was powerful enough to create innumerable diseases with piles of medical proof, then I was also powerful enough to create something different - the life of my dreams!

Almost 4 years later, I have done just that. Since regaining my health, I have been able to travel throughout the United States and Europe, speaking and teaching. A few years ago, my family and I were able to live in South Africa to do mission work. And now, I live in Maui - one of the most desirable vacation destinations in the world! I have my own FasterEFT practice, and I am happier and healthier than ever. I have even been able to influence my own family with FasterEFT. My mother has overcome debilitating addiction, my brother has overcome years of heartache and pain, and my husband has found freedom from crippling self-doubt. I have helped countless people find peace through FasterEFT.

The power to heal was mine the whole time!

I am living the BEST life! My children have their mother, and my husband has his wife. I have been given so much. And to think, the power to heal was mine the whole time!

Heather Bolton McKean is a women's ministry leader, a missionary, and a Level 4 FasterEFT practitioner. She lives in Hawaii with her family, and since her healing through FasterEFT, she has travelled the world ministering to others.

Heather had dealt with numerous diseases and pain from a young age. She was well-acquainted with Western Medicine and consulted many specialists for various illnesses. By 2012, she had tried EVERYTHING, but was sicker than ever. She was wallowing in a diagnosis of Lyme disease with multiple co-infections, chronic fatigue syndrome, fibromyalgia, endometriosis, thunderclap headaches/migraine disorder, POTS, Hashimoto's disease, anaemia, ankylosing spondylitis, adrenal fatigue, rheumatoid arthritis, Reiter's syndrome, degenerative disc disease, renal hyper-filtration, intestinal dysbiosis, and more. It seems impossible, but she has the blood work, MRIs, CT scans, echocardiograms and all other tests to 'prove' it.

Through her many years of illness, she became acquainted with nearly every modality of holistic healing and had tried many of them without experiencing relief. By the Grace of God, she was told about tapping methodologies and stumbled upon FasterEFT on YouTube. Within 2 weeks, she was on the way to changing her life when she attended a FasterEFT Transformational Retreat and Level 1 Practitioner Training. The rest is history!

Heather feels enormously blessed to be able to share her story and healing journey with others.

Website:

www.tapintou.com

Email:

TapIntoU@icloud.com

MauiMindChange@icloud.com

Facebook:

www.facebook.com/TapIntoU/

YouTube:

Heather McKean TakeCaptiveEveryThought

The Business Comes First

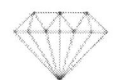

Ilka Oster

My dad doesn't want kids - but after 4 years of marriage to my mum, something changes and my mum gives birth to me. Ilka Julia is the name I am given. My sister arrives 3 years later. We are the fifth generation to be born into our sawmilling family. When I am 4 years old, we move to a new town to run another sawmill my family has purchased. My grandparents join us.

The business comes first.

'The business comes first,' is my dad's mantra throughout my life. We have a very comfortable life and are reminded constantly in many different ways that this good life comes at the price of hardship and stress. My dad begins taking Valium in heavy dosages when I am young, and this continues in one form or another for most of his life.

From early in my dad's life, my grandfather 'goes quiet' and literally stops talking altogether. He is taken to Melbourne and given shock therapy. When I am young, I see how hard this is on my mum, dad, and grandmother. I wonder why this happens.

One day, dad is supposed to pick me up from school, but he forgets. Standing outside the school for what seems like eternity to a 5-year-old, I am scared and extremely sad. I had been excited about my dad picking me up. It is the first and last time he is ever asked to do this. A school friend's mum rescues me, and when she takes me back to his office I am brushed aside. He has more important things to do than talk to me.

By age 11, I am off to boarding school, where I spend most of the next 6 years of my life. At boarding school, there are a myriad of unwritten rules governing everything from what you should wear to how you should speak. I miss home when I first get there, but I get used to it. I love to try all the different activities and relish the opportunity to play lots of different sports. I am very glad to have my sense of humour at boarding school. My ability to laugh at myself and not take things so seriously helps me deal with my feelings of awkwardness and 'not fitting in.' I make many lifelong friends, and all in all it is a positive experience.

Growing up I hear family stories of near bankruptcy, hardship, and stress to keep our businesses going. This makes me very determined to show my dad that I can work physically hard and be financially independent.

During my twenties I live in Melbourne, working various jobs. I work hard and do lots of overtime. I always feel so proud to ring my dad and tell him about this. I share my ideas about my work and the businesses I work for. These are treasured conversations with my dad.

I decide to move to Darwin, nearly 3000 kilometres from my home town in the Riverina of New South Wales where I have grown up. I love the expanse and ruggedness of the Northern Territory. Whilst working in

Darwin, I meet my husband, Simon. A year later we move back to my home. I am excited to marry my best friend and become Mrs Ilka Oster. Our oldest daughter, Ellie, arrives 2 years later. Then Sam and Ruby join our family over the next 5 years. Simon and I spend 15 years running the logging operation of the family sawmill. I help with the bookwork and educate my 3 kids at home.

After moving home from Darwin, I experience the lowest times in my whole life. I constantly beat myself up in my mind. I can never live up to the high expectations I have of myself. I am scared of ending up like my dad and grandfather. I start to devour books about health and self-development and try many natural alternative health therapies. I start learning that it's possible to have a different life. The bad feelings and thoughts get more manageable - but they still nag away at me.

Throughout the years, my dad's pattern of being on a high one week followed by sick and depressed the next continues. The father I look up to so much is brilliant – yet he is also alcoholic and sometimes angry and depressed. The strained relationship with him is not easy for any of us. I am desperate to find ways to deal with my response to his moods and alcoholism. I keep wondering if there is an easier more peaceful way to be in life.

In 2009 the government closes our logging areas, and we are left without a business. Simon and I decide to move our family to Queensland. As we prepare to leave, my dad has many trips to the hospital with emphysema and infection. He has been a chain smoker for most of his life. On several occasions, the doctors tell us he is going to die - but he holds on. Heavy doses of morphine and plenty of alcohol take away his pain. Then the week after we move, he dies with my mum and sister holding his hands.

I love him so much. He is a big part of me, my determination, my passion, the way I seek answers, and how I think outside the box. He has also been my greatest challenge. I carry many old hurts that are still raw and unhealed. I am celebrating his life and am also sad, angry, resentful, and filled with guilt. After my father dies, I somehow discover FasterEFT online. I am instantly intrigued and attend a seminar with Robert G Smith in Brisbane. I am so happy and so in awe of what this amazing modality can do. The changes I notice in myself are incredible to say the least. The constant anxiety has disappeared, and I am a new person. I have made peace with my past. The best part is I am empowered to keep expanding, growing, and feeling better each day.

> I had to make huge changes to my beliefs.
> FasterEFT has made this possible.

Three years later, my life is different in every way. There have been huge, massive changes inside of me. I am so much calmer and happier, and I am fulfilling a lifelong dream of running my own business. For this to happen, I had to make huge changes to my beliefs. FasterEFT has made this possible.

To honour my past, my vision is to bridge the gap between the business world and our emotional intelligence – so that health, loving relationships, abundance, and financial and business success can become mutually INCLUSIVE! This is my dream, and it's becoming a reality.

Ilka lives on the Sunshine Coast in Australia and is a Level 3 FasterEFT practitioner. Her company is called 'Growing Inner Wealth,' and she specializes in working with people who want to 'power up' their inner wealth and let go of the beliefs that hold them back from reaching their full potential in every aspect of life.

Ilka works with clients in her office on Queensland's Sunshine Coast. She also uses Skype to work with clients throughout Australia and internationally.

Ilka firmly believes that it's important to challenge erroneous beliefs about money, such as, 'stress and hardship equals success,' 'you can't have good health, good relationships and a successful business,' 'a woman's place is in the home,' and 'my business is more important than my family or me.' She offers a '30 Day Facebook Challenge' every month that connects like-minded people, creates awareness of unconscious money programs, gives tools to change mental money programs, and helps people to work out what they most value and want in life - so they can make it happen!

Ilka believes in helping people to strengthen beliefs that serve their highest good.

Website:

www.growinginnerwealth.com

Email:

ilka@growinginnerwealth.com

Facebook Page:

www.facebook.com/growinginnerwealth

Never Give Up!

Jacqueline Tipping-Schutt

I was a juggling superwoman

So, there I was in 2008, living my very, very busy life. I was a juggling superwoman: wife, mother, executive, studying, moving house, working out, travelling, and generally living in the very fast lane! Then one day it all came tumbling down.

I went to work feeling a bit under the weather. I had been pushing through this feeling for a while. By lunch time I had to go home - and I never returned. Ever. I thought it was a virus and it would get better. It did for a while, but then it relapsed again and again. The days off work turned into weeks off work, and then months and then years. I lay in my bed unable to function properly. Everything was a massive effort. After being very healthy all my life I became very, very sick.

Finally, I was diagnosed with Chronic Fatigue Syndrome

It was so frustrating, and I couldn't understand what was happening to me. I went from doctor to doctor, and the time marched on. Finally, I was diagnosed with CFS (Chronic Fatigue Syndrome), and my world changed forever.

> It was pure torture and hell,
> and I couldn't see a good way out.

There seemed to be no way out! I was bedridden, seriously incapacitated, and couldn't work. I could hardly interact with anyone, and everything left me feeling drained and exhausted. My digestive system was in a poor state. I was losing weight, had no energy, was limp, and felt very trapped. There were many days when I felt desperate, lost, depressed, hopeless, and seeing no future for myself. It felt like a continual roller coaster. It was pure torture and hell, and I couldn't see a good way out.

Somehow I managed to hang on, one minute at a time, one day at a time, one week at a time. Something deep inside of me told me I had to be open, that I had to look for other answers, and that I could not give up. I realised quite early on that if I was going to heal then it was going to have to be up to me! Having exhausted the path of traditional western medicine, where I was offered antidepressants and sleeping pills and little else, I commenced a long journey of self-discovery and searching for the way out of this unacceptable life. I went to many naturopaths, Traditional Chinese medicine doctors, acupuncturists, meditations groups, clairvoyants, sound therapy, colour therapy, Reiki, essential oil therapy, plus many more alternative and spiritual practices. I also studied and became a practitioner, myself, in many of these holistic and complementary modalities.

I kept moving forward. Over time I attended numerous appointments and many workshops. I read a huge number of books and, of course, researched and read widely on the internet. Many of these activities contributed greatly to my very slow improvement. I met many earth angels along the way to whom I will be eternally grateful. Quite a few of them helped to save my life. In time, I was about 50 percent better, but I still lead a very limited life and had to carefully plan how I would use my precious energy.

My inner voice was telling me to be open, even though my logical brain and limiting beliefs sometimes dominated.

Eventually, through a holistic support group I attended, I learned about FasterEFT, developed by Robert Smith. I didn't take it up right away, however, because I was still using some of the other methods I had already learned. At some point, though, I started exploring FasterEFT and was quickly convinced of its fast and effective results. My inner voice was telling me to be open, even though my logical brain and limiting beliefs sometimes dominated.

One day a fellow CFS sufferer mentioned that evidence showed very few people ever recover from CFS, and she had resolved to accept her condition. I turned to her and said, 'And we will be among the ones that do recover!' It turned out that we did! But at this point I was actually unsure of how much better I could really get with FasterEFT. Still, I was determined to find my way out of this health and life crisis, even though I was currently 'stuck' and could not seem to move into the last part of my recovery.

With my next big step, however, I saw the problem completely resolve. As a result of some of my spiritual practices I wanted to go to India to the Oneness Ashram. Well, part of me wanted to go, and part of me was scared silly. I was still very unwell, and wanting to going to India . . . really, what was I thinking! But I knew I had to go. I deeply wanted to keep moving forward and started doing more and more FasterEFT. I began to see and feel the results in my mind and body. Something was shifting. With the further help of my dear friend Di Downward – a FasterEFT practitioner – I was able to tap out the fear and many other challenges to enable me to travel to India, where I received much relief from my symptoms. By this stage I was about 70 percent better.

I began to see how I had suppressed many emotions in my life.

I continued to practice FasterEFT, and I continued to improve on all levels. I completed the 7-day free online course that Robert offers, and I attended FasterEFT workshops with Judy Timperon here in South Australia, where I live. The more I did FasterEFT, the more I realised the power of this technique. It was proving highly effective, swift, and empowering. I began to see how I had suppressed many emotions in my life. I saw, too, how my early formed beliefs had shaped my life and held me back. I started to become freer and freer.

In 2014, I attended the full Level 1 FasterEFT training in person. I didn't know if I could do it. How could I pace myself for 7 days of training in a row? How could I manage? I tapped on this fear to set myself up as best I could. In the breaks, I went out to my car to rest. When I came home I rested immediately, as I was wiped out. Thankfully I was loved and fully supported by my husband in these efforts. I continued with my FasterEFT studies – trading sessions with 'tapping buddies' and also paying for sessions.

Along the way, I had some big breakthroughs with some amazing practitioners, including Deirdre, Judy, Debra, Pam, and all my amazing tapping buddies – such as, Arunika Hamden, who always made me laugh. My health improved further. I completed Level 2 FasterEFT in 2015, received more sessions, and gave more sessions. I set up a business called the 'Joy of Living,' which reflected exactly what I was feeling and what I wanted others to feel. In 2016, I completed my Level 3 practitioner training.

Like a hungry caterpillar, I was ready for change.

My journey with this illness lasted about 6 ½ years, and I am over it now. It was a long, long road. I was determined. Like a hungry caterpillar, I was ready for change. Slowly I began to transform my life. Sometimes I slipped and returned to old ways of living and thinking. But I knew I needed to change my life or not have one. Gradually, I became more aware of myself, my beliefs, and my actions. I now realise negative automatic behaviours I had not even considered before. I am less reactive, although I am still a work in progress.

My husband knows enough to remind me to tap sometimes on things that bother me, even if those 'things' are him! If we disagree, I used to be able to hold a grudge or work on the silent treatment for quite some time. Things are different now. I'm able to process things quicker, and I'm more honest and able to express my feelings in a healthy manner. Some of my earlier beliefs came from wanting to be 'a good girl' or 'a pleaser' - often at my own expense. I can see this clearly now and have worked on breaking through these limiting beliefs. I am grateful to be free of many of these now. We all have so many, most often imprinted when we are very young. I can see how many limiting beliefs, fears, and other issues led to my illness and life crisis. I had lost part of me, my true essence, and my joy. But I found my way back to me - the real authentic me. My relationship with myself has changed. I can see me more clearly now. I understand me more. I value and love myself more. As a result, I think I am a better human being. It is OK to be authentic, have emotions, and express them. I am still a work in progress, and that's OK.

My life has changed forever. I - and indeed my husband and family - now lead very different, better, richer, and more joyful lives. My family have benefited from all the education. They are more empowered, and see the value in FasterEFT sessions. They are reaping the rewards in their lives, as well.

> I know that this is how life is meant to be lived.

I know that this is how life is meant to be lived. I love life. I love spending time with my family and friends. I walk every day. I enjoy reading, studying, working with others, travelling, and 'being.' I transformed many beliefs along the way. I am much more aware, much freer, liberated, and confident that I have tools to assist me when things come up.

What if it could be easier than you think?

Although I no longer suffer from CFS (yah!), I can see now that the illness and situation I found myself in was actually a gift - in an unusual wrapping paper - and it could be the same for you! Your wrapping paper may be different, but what if it were possible to help yourself? What if it could be easier than you think?

I now truly believe anything is possible. I am so grateful for everything and everyone in my life. I have met some amazing people. I have been transformed from surviving to thriving. Part of my mission, passion, and JOY now lies in using the things I have learnt to make it easier for others to find THEIR JOY . . . so they too can live, grow, be healthy, be abundant, be vibrant, and lead JOYFUL lives. It can happen for you. As Winston Churchill said, 'Never give up!'

I am truly filled with JOY. I'm on top of the world! I wish the same for you!

Jacqueline Tipping-Schutt is a Transformation Guide who conducts private sessions in person in Adelaide, Australia, and via Skype nationally and internationally. Her practice is an accumulation of many years of experience in the worlds of education, corporate business, and complementary healing. She combines all her personal skills and knowledge from her own health crisis, in an easy form, to facilitate healing and freedom at the deepest level. She also offers online group webinars and courses on a wide range of helpful key topics.

Jacqueline is passionate about inspiring and assisting others to learn, grow, and lead more authentic, joyful lives. Her approach with clients is engaging, creating a safe environment as she skilfully guides them to make peace with the past, change the present, and create a more joyful future.

Many of her clients have experienced freedom from a variety of challenges including: chronic health conditions, anxiety, depression, fears, weight challenges, cravings and addictions, grief and loss, feeling stuck, trauma, relationship problems, insomnia, performance, and more. Jacqueline is currently facilitating a committee with Robert Smith, founder of FasterEFT, and practitioners from around the world who are working to improve the modality's outcomes, training structure, processes, and much more.

Website:
www.joyofliving.net.au

Email:
Jacqueline@joyofliving.net.au

Opening the Door to the World of the Mind

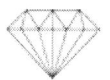

Jean Erickson

Coming from a small family of three, I was the oldest child and only girl. My childhood was traumatic and fraught with abuse, abandonment, and attachment issues. With few friends but lots of brains and ambition, I set out to prove my worth.

My journey began with a career in graphic design and marketing in which I continued to climb the ladder of success - with greater and greater responsibilities and pressure. Life for me was a continuous stream of deadlines and projects, taking up more and more hours of the day. I married young and had two children, continuing my 'career woman' path even while knowing that I wished for more time with my family. Opposing desires created internal conflict, so I learned to bury my emotions. Like many Americans, I ended up taking antidepressants to help keep up the pace. Finally, I achieved my dream job as an art director for a software company based in France. Enjoying international travel and enduring unrelenting work, I continued to give my all, and then my body began to break down.

Eventually the perfect storm hit. A pair of layoffs took the sparkle off of careerism. Feeling more cynical, and also deeply hurt, I chose to go into business for myself. More deadlines, projects, and success followed, but I was reaching the end of my rope. A move to a different city, the loss of most of my clients, both children leaving home, and my husband working 10 to 11 hours a day all combined to leave me feeling alone and empty.

I kept getting sicker and sicker.

Then I began to have alarming physical symptoms. One day - with my heart pounding in my chest, my arms going numb, and feeling shaky and weak - I was convinced I was having a heart attack. I went to the emergency room and had lots of tests done. Their conclusion: 'Your heart looks OK, and we have no idea what caused the symptoms.' I kept getting sicker and sicker.

Traditional medicine did not understand what was going on with me. Eventually I found an integrative practitioner that recognized the symptoms and did some tests, finding at that point that my cortisol levels were 4 to 5 times the normal levels which was keeping me from sleeping and my body from repairing. Eventually these high levels crashed, and it was determined that I now was enduring adrenal fatigue. My integrative practitioner gave me a book on the topic with instructions to rest (I couldn't do anything else!) and told me I needed to get my cortisol levels down. She had no suggestions as to how.

I went looking for answers. I began implementing suggestions from the work of Dr. Diana Schwarzbein. I also continued to work with traditional doctors, but all the traditional resources I normally counted on had failed. A pretty logical thinker, I had generally dismissed alternative medicine as 'hokey,' 'new age,' or 'illogical' - at best wishful thinking, and, at worst, a scam.

I felt very foolish,
but had a bit of success with it, enough to keep trying.

Feeling worse every day, I was willing to try something, anything, new - especially if there were no chemical side effects or high costs involved. A friend on an exercise chat board suggested I try an emotional healing modality she had heard about. I felt very foolish, but had a bit of success with it, enough to keep trying. Then I found formal clinical studies documenting that a related modality could reduce cortisol levels. I continued working on myself and got more results, but they were spotty. Still, I was better off than before.

The belief system seemed more logical, as it was based on
how the brain and body work.

As I was beginning to see some improvements, I saw a Meetup group being advertised in my city for 'FasterEFT.' I was so excited at just the idea of getting together with others who knew what I was doing and who would not ridicule it. At my first meeting it became clear that there were significant differences between this modality and the others I had tried. And I liked those differences! The belief system seemed more logical, as it was based on how the brain and body work. And it took much of the guessing element out of the practice of it! And it was faster! I started to hope again.

> After one session, the phobia was 85 to 90 percent gone!

After a summer of attending Meetup groups, I decided to come to a FasterEFT Transformational Weekend in October of 2012 – hosted by Robert G. Smith, the originator of the method. Much of what was taught I had already learned, but the experience of tapping on myself for two days straight was enlightening. I did not get to sit in Robert's 'magic chair' for my major issue ('political phobia,' which had me enduring panic attacks everywhere and all the time). Where can you go to avoid politics in October? After the weekend, a practitioner came up, offered me her card, and said, 'Give me a call if you want to take care of that issue.' I called a week later and scheduled a Skype appointment. After one session, the phobia was 85 to 90 percent gone! I was able to have a political discussion with my son – and no fear! Wow!

> I had found what I was born to do.

I decided soon after to attend Level I Training the following February. By the end of the week, I felt that I had found what I was born to do. I took the course straight through with the intention of attaining Level IV. I received my Advanced, Level 4 certification in 2014.

My experience of FasterEFT is different from many others. I cannot always tell when changes are happening. I don't always 'feel the feeling' or get a 'clear picture' as I recall a memory. One time, while working on a very big issue, I did feel a lot of very intense emotion. During the process, the emotion lessened and cleared. Immediately afterwards I laid down and felt tingling sensations running up my arms and legs toward my heart. This is more the exception than the rule in my experience.

One strange side effect of FasterEFT is that after years of 'no feeling,' I am now ticklish again! And I notice changes after the fact. For example, weeks after clearing a childhood memory that involved me being strangled while singing to my doll, I found myself singing out loud in a public group. I now had no fear - only joy!

When you change yourself,
that your relationships with other people change.

Over time I have learned what works for me, but my clearest touchstone for knowing that FasterEFT is working is how my husband and children react. 'It definitely has created changes,' they've said. Even my relationship with my parents has changed significantly. I am now able to meet them 'in the present' without all the issues of the past coming up. It is true that when you change yourself, that your relationships with other people change too. This has affected the family dynamic significantly!

In addition to your relationships with people changing, FasterEFT can clear even spiritual relationships. My relationship with God has also been restored and healed. For this I am extremely thankful. It is a source of peace, hope, and strength for me.

I enjoy my life now. I have been lifting weights, walking, hiking, and pursuing the life I want. In the last year I have taken driving trips totaling over 9000 miles. A year ago I went to the East Coast, visited clients and a friend, and partnered with another practitioner to do a week of 'crossfire' FasterEFT sessions. Then I drove down the Blue Ridge Parkway and nearly 1500 miles home. At the beginning of the year I drove to California for training and took side trips to visit relatives and fellow FasterEFT practitioners, as well as enjoying Route 1, the Redwoods, and the Grand Canyon. I love having the strength and courage to travel.

Sometimes old issues rise up for deeper healing.
But now I have resources to handle what life brings me!

My life today is not perfect. There have been challenges and things happening in the world beyond my control. Sometimes old issues rise up for deeper healing. But now I have resources to handle what life brings me! My personal work includes prayer, and I have expanded my FasterEFT coaching to occasionally include the work of Dr. John Sarno, Self-Directed Neuroplasticity, NLP, and other methods.

We can change our lives
by changing our thoughts and emotions.

I am thankful now for that perfect storm of events that at the time was so painful and frightening. I'm thankful because it brought me to the point of realizing that we can change our lives by changing our thoughts and emotions. The world of the mind has been opened to me, and that door can never be closed.

Jean Erickson lives in the United States and is a Level 4 FasterEFT practitioner and personal growth coach who founded her company think.feel.change! in 2013.

After 30 years in the high-powered corporate world working in graphic design and marketing, she now brings her creativity and analytical skills to help individuals change their thoughts and emotions for the better. Her clients are empowered to relieve stress, anxiety, fear, phobias, painful memories, limiting beliefs, grief, sadness and other emotions underlying stress-related physical symptoms. Her company boasts an international client list that draws from countries including the United Kingdom, Portugal, Austria, Hungary, Saudi Arabia, and India. In her home country, her clients hail from Washington state to Washington DC, and most states in between.

Jean believes that our memories and experiences (the inner voices and input from other sources) plus our emotions and physical sensations create our perceptions. These perceptions can be the source of much of our stress. Her mission is to help empower clients to take control of their thoughts and feelings, allowing their experiences of life to change dramatically.

Jean has helped hundreds of clients struggling with fears and phobias, grief and loss, and chronic pain and stress. Her speciality is helping create change for 'tough' or 'resistant' clients. She takes the time to understand how a specific client's memories work, and works within that person's belief system and worldview.

Jean primarily uses FasterEFT but is also familiar with (and, when appropriate, utilizes) a variety of modalities, including the TMS principles of Dr. John Sarno, Self-Directed Neuroplasticity, Ericksonian hypnosis, and Neuro-Linguistic Programming. She is passionately interested in and continually researches the brain, learning, and neuroplasticity. She has taught a popular online course on the subject entitled 'NeuroPLUSticity.' Her clients have described her as 'terrifically talented,' 'amazing,' and the 'ultimate professional with a compassionate heart.'

Website:

www.thinkfeelchange.com

can you Believe it !

Keep it Light and Make Them Laugh!

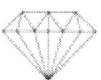

Jeannette van Uffelen

In the more than thirty years that I worked as a social worker, a trainer, and a coach, I also educated myself in many philosophies, alternative health practices, and healing modalities. I have learned and practiced acupuncture and Shiatsu therapy, to name just a few modalities I know. I have read many motivational books and seen all the inspiring movies, like *What the Bleep Do We Know!?* I've listened to and read many hours of Louise Hay, Wayne Dyer, Tony Robbins, and more. I have even done rituals with shamans from the Brazilian rainforest. In all this study and work, I was learning and changing—and all together, these methods and resources made my life better. But maybe I was always searching for just the 'right' thing for me. This is my story about how I found FasterEFT and how it helped me get to where I am now.

'Those born a penny
are never meant to become a quarter.'

I've had many jobs, experiences, and changes in my life. I left home at age 18, just three months after I started my first real job. I had no idea what work I wanted to do or could do, so I took the first job I found - just because I wanted to be independent. At home we had no big expectations and no big dreams. In The Netherlands, we have an old saying that 'those born a penny are never meant to become a quarter.' In my family, people never aimed above their current circumstances.

I've always wanted to help people, and I continued to train myself to do that while working at every job I ever had. For instance, at the age of 20, after holding an office job and then bartending for a while, I started working in a psychiatric hospital and also began studying to be a social worker. But by age 35, after 15 years of working in all kinds of crisis situations—like domestic violence, abuse, and addictions—I was fed up with hearing about human struggles.

So I changed professions to become an Information & Communication Technician (ICT) specialist. I'm not the kind of person who wants to sit by myself at a computer all day long, however, so I soon changed professions once more and became a computer trainer, which allowed me to work with people again. From that job, I progressed to giving many kinds of training, especially in personal development and life coaching. I even had my own training and coaching business for 10 years.

Something had to change.

Although people were happy with the work I did, I wasn't enjoying it, and it wasn't emotionally rewarding. By 2013, my knees were overloaded, and I needed crutches to walk. Something had to change. Since I had done all kinds of self-healing in the past, I felt sure that I could heal myself, and I set out to do that. So I started the year 2014 by watching an online 'Summit' of many self-healing methods given by Hay House. After watching different practitioners, I began to 'Google' various modalities, and one result that came up was 'Robert Smith' and 'FasterEFT.'

This was pure and real.

The videos I found of Robert had been recorded at Habilitat, the drug treatment center in Hawaii, and these videos made so much sense to me. What I liked most was that Robert and the clients were just sitting there in T-shirts, sweating and talking. There were no polished ads, no perfect scenery, and he was not on the *New York Times* Bestsellers' List. This was pure and real. Robert was real.

I watched one video after another, I tapped along, and I started to feel better. Not only did my knees improve, but I solved other life issues. So after about 2 months, I decided to buy the home-study course, and in the same week I booked my first Level 1 live seminar in Budapest, Hungary, which I attended in April 2014.

In Budapest, there were fifty of us from all over Europe, along with a few people from the USA. And by tapping on each other and spending time in the wellness sauna of the hotel, we created friendships. After coming home, I started to swap sessions with some people I met there, and we continued to improve our FasterEFT skills. We shared our deepest secrets, helped each other release all kinds of stuff, and were each other's guinea pigs to become better and better practitioners of FasterEFT. I was on fire and had set my goals: (1) be a Level 3 practitioner by the end of the year, and (2) volunteer as a FasterEFT practitioner at Habilitat.

I live in a multicultural city. I already had many years of working with all kinds of people - from all different backgrounds, all walks of life, all continents in the world, all levels of education, and all ages. I love to help people, and I felt that this tool, FasterEFT, was really working. And doing this work with addicts, I believed, would be the ultimate proof it worked. I wanted to experience and learn that myself, so I applied to Robert by email.

In 2015 while I was in Athens at a Level 2 live seminar, Robert invited me to go to Habilitat. So I flew to Hawaii to do FasterEFT with people I hoped would really benefit from it. Meanwhile I had closed my coaching business after 10 years, was in debt, and had had no income for more than a year. But I was giving sessions to everyone and anyone who came near to me because I wanted to learn and experience.

I've become a much easier and kinder person to myself.

I had great results and loved to give sessions in person and via Skype, so I started to ask money for the sessions and built up a new business. Receiving many hours of sessions by fellow practitioners ('tapping buddies') and also higher-level practitioners helped me to get rid of all that was holding me back from being as great as I can be. It gave me confidence to start a new business again. But this time I moved forward and did things in the way I myself wanted - and not the way others expected me to do them. So this time creating a business has been much simpler, and the way I go about my work is easier and faster. That's because I've become a much easier and kinder person to myself and to all around me.

> I was in great debt last year, but not anymore.

My life today is a big adventure. I feel healthy and I am in good shape. I had been on diets most of my life, but I'm not anymore. I just listen to myself and to my body, and I eat as I want without feeling limited. I'm doing well and making money. I was in great debt last year, but not anymore. My work is a joy because I love to do it and it is so effective. The office I work in is in a beautiful spot, where I cooperate with colleagues who employ various modalities (psychotherapy, bodywork, etc). When they have clients who get 'stuck,' they send them to me, and mostly one session is enough for a breakthrough.

> Keep it light and make them laugh.

This year, 2016, I was back in Habilitat. As a FasterEFT practitioner, I want to be thorough, fast, and deep - as well as focused, empathetic, relaxed, and funny. My motto is 'Keep it light and make them laugh,' because I've experienced that deep laughter is the best 'trance breaker' during the FasterEFT session.

Today I am more at peace - with myself, life, and the world - than ever before. In the last year I've build up a new business and focused on my favorite activities: being me, spending time with my loved ones, being a FasterEFT practitioner and trainer, singing in a choir, painting icons, building websites, and living a healthy life. I've built a new international career and love to work with people from all over the planet.

Often we can make our lives so much better and easier than they were, and I'm happy to have found a way to really help and give a tool to everyone who wants it. Thanks to Robert Smith, to all the FasterEFT practitioners I've worked with, and to Deirdre Maguire, who is a good and very funny practitioner to work with and who gave me the opportunity to share my story.

Jeannette van Uffelen lives in The Netherlands and is a stress release expert and FasterEFT advanced practitioner (Level 4). She specializes in working with people who have stress issues, PTSD, and trauma. She works with individuals as well as groups. Jeanette has extensive experience with addiction, and with people on substance addiction as well as addiction to certain behaviours. Many female clients find her because she's known for her skills of inspiring and empowering women in a natural, practical, and humoristic way.

On the personal side, Jeannette is an icon painter in the Orthodox tradition, with a more artistic than religious motivation, although it is a silent meditative way of painting. She likes churches for the sounds, the smells, and the art. Her real church is the sea, and she swims in the North Sea all through the year. She practices yoga, Pilates, and BodyPump weekly; and in the city where she lives, she prefers to travel on her old-fashioned bicycle. It's faster, cheaper, and healthier.

Jeannette is often singing, and the neighbours do approve. She sings alto in a chamber choir and has been the lead singer in a band. She likes to express herself creatively and has learnt many ways to do it, because she just loves to make things. She loves to challenge herself by finding practical solutions while making repairs or doing handicrafts or art. Jeannette is the creator and webmaster of websites for her choir and her icon teacher.

Jeannette's greatest accomplishment is being the mother of her daughter Litô. "The last 21 years with this amazing person and beautiful soul have been a great joy and continue to be." Jeannette loves being a wanderer and a traveller, discovering people and places. At the same time, she is always happy to be back home again.

Websites:
- www.skillstochange.eu
- www.jeannettevanuffelen.com

Address:
The Hague, The Netherlands
+31613223075

Skypename:
jeannettevanuffelen

Email:

yes@skillstochange.eu

info@jeannettevanuffelen.com

YouTube Channels:

Jeannette van Uffelen SkillsToChange

Skills to Change Europe

LinkedIn

https://www.linkedin.com/in/jeannettevanuffelen/

Facebook:

https://www.facebook.com/jeannettevanuff

Twitter:

https://twitter.com/JeannetteVitaal/

Pinterest:

https://nl.pinterest.com/JeannetteUff/

Google+

https://plus.google.com/+JeannettevanUffelenSkillsToChange

https://plus.google.com/u/0/+Jean

can you Believe it !

Drugs Were My Best Friend

Jeff Nash

Although I had maintained complete abstinence for nearly 16 years, the love for the drug never left me.

My name is Jeff Nash, former drug addict for many years. I was offered an opportunity to work with Deirdre to help me overcome some of the baggage associated with 14 years of heroin addiction.

Having worked with traditional EFT practitioners, I wasn't expecting very much. Although I had maintained complete abstinence for nearly 16 years, the love for the drug never left me. There were so many references that freedom from the feelings seemed impossible. Although I had managed to tough it out and create a good life for myself, I still had a hard time when I would see a syringe. I felt sick at my stomach and cringed in fear.

I was very skeptical.

Deirdre took the time to explain why it was important to change my internal reference so that those feelings could never be triggered again. I must admit I was very skeptical. I arrived for a one on one session with an open mind. I immediately noticed that Deirdre had a gift for quickly building rapport. I felt comfortable being honest with her.

She began to work her magic.

After the initial intake she began to work her magic. She told me to go ahead and feel it for the last time.

Drugs were my best friend.
Heroin had been the only thing dependable in my life.

To my surprise, she produced a syringe, a spoon and a lighter and placed them on the table. My body reacted and she started leading me through the ritual of using drugs.

There were so many references, feelings, and memories after years of drug use. Drugs were my best friend through so many hard times. It was always there, doing what is was supposed to do. Heroin had been the only thing dependable in my life. After about an hour I realized that my body was no longer reacting to the syringe. I couldn't even bring the memories back into focus.

> Not only was it gone, but I could actually pick up the needle and play with it without even a hint of reaction.

By the end of the second hour I was astonished. Not only was it gone, but I could actually pick up the needle and play with it without even a hint of reaction. It seemed too good to be true. Surely this is only temporary! It'll come back a few days from now! It didn't.

That two hour session was nearly 4 years ago. Never again has my body responded the same way again. I've seen people using drugs a few times since then but somehow it's just not the same anymore. There is no sick stomach or sweaty palms. It's all just gone!

> To say that this was a life changing event would be an understatement.

To say that this was a life changing event would be an understatement.

Deirdre cleared my mind of a lifetime of garbage in just two hours. I have continued to do sessions with her through the years on various other subjects and she seems to always know exactly what to do. I would recommend Ms. Maguire without hesitation for anyone dealing with any issue that causes unwanted emotions. From addiction, grief and loss, relationships, or anger issues, she has helped me with them all. She has become the "go to" person in my life when I need help. I am always astonished at how quickly she can have me feeling better.

Jeff is the Executive Director at Habilitat Inc. Drugs and Alcohol Rehabilitation Program in Hawaii.

Website:

www.habilitat.com

it was important. The loss of friendships hit me most acutely, as well as feeling so alone. Scott's labouring took him away from me for sometimes weeks at a time. He is not a labourer by choice, and this hit him very hard too. But he did what had to be done. We both did.

For the first time I understand why people can kill themselves.

Walking out of the lawyer's office one day Scott said, 'For the first time I understand why people can kill themselves.' 'What do you mean?' I replied. Scott went on to elaborate on the 'family curse' he felt. When his grandmother wrote her family history, she refused to write the history of her husband's family because of the multitude of tragedies that had occurred in his family line. Scott's mother always felt he had escaped this as he is naturally optimistic, like her.

Scott's great-grandfather was the first to suicide. Then his father and uncle suicided when Scott was in his early 20s. His younger brother made several attempts before his early death. So much tragedy happened in one family.

The 'curse' the family felt had been put onto them.

FasterEFT to the rescue! Scott became my 'client,' and I worked on many memories with him. The deaths and suicides of his close family members, the late night phone calls from his brother when he had over-imbibed, and the many childhood memories of trauma with his alcoholic father were all brought up and addressed with the FasterEFT process. We even went back into his family heritage and changed the memory of his great-grandfather's suicide and the 'curse' the family felt had been put onto them. The reason: his grieving great-grandmother had been blaming her husband for the death of their son, and this had precipitated his suicide. We made peace with Scott's heritage – and as we did this, I saw so much positive change in Scott.

Recently I have read Mark Wolynn's book, *It Didn't Start with You: How Inherited Family Trauma Shapes Who We Are*. This book has given me new insights into healing the past. Many clients do come to me with inherited family trauma, and FasterEFT has been the tool I have used to help them make peace with their past. With the new science of epigenetics, we have greater understandings of how trauma is trapped in family memories.

Scott had many happy memories with his father, but also many unhappy memories with him – including times his father 'stole' from him. An inheritance came to Scott from his mother's side of the family, and his father took it from him.

Another example: Scott had saved so hard to buy his first motorbike, and his father sold it when Scott was away from home and used the money to put towards a tractor. Scott had worked for his father on the farm for 2 years without payment – and had kept records of this - but his father destroyed his record book. Is it any wonder that he had been recently frauded? This had been an ongoing theme in his life from his teen years.

That old memory was no longer serving him

These are only a portion of the memories we tapped on, utilising Scott's FasterEFT 'peace journal.' He made peace with the past! He recreated a new life for himself in his mind, which then became reflected in his present life. We went into each memory, made peace with all the characters in the memory and changed the memory.

For example, instead of Scott arriving home to find his new bike sold and his father with a new tractor, we tapped away the hurts and betrayal and reimprinted Scott having his bike and his father also having a tractor. After all, that old memory was no longer serving him – he let it go and recreated what he wanted.

This now became his new, real memory. True, this new memory never happened, but that old memory was not true anymore either. It's over, and the only place it was now happening was in his mind, so he made peace with it. As he changed what was happening in his mind, his whole life began to improve.

As a result of consistently doing this work as anything came up for him, Scott gradually began working in a career area that was more suited to him, and he continues to thrive. We are back travelling, he goes on motorbike adventures, and abundance in its many forms is back in our lives. For instance, we are not far off being able to purchase a new home. We are currently living in a wonderful home, so when we buy our house, we may not even live in it as we are so comfortable and happy where we are!

As for myself, I always thought I came from that 'perfect family.' My parents are still alive, and I have been blessed with an abundance of love and support. I knew I had to dig deeper to address issues that were affecting our lives. I decided to tap on my grandfather's history. He had arrived home from the war, invested his money, and lost the lot. He was never able to recover from this. I realised I was reliving what had happened to my grandfather. I felt this most acutely – so I cleaned it up, and re-created a new memory. This was easy to do. I had a good idea how my grandfather was feeling, as I was feeling this myself! It was so easy to trade places with him and make peace with everything within me. I then created a new memory where my grandfather reaped the rewards of his investments, and owned a beautiful mansion.

Within 3 months, Scott and I were living in the beautiful mansion we now call home. Coincidence? Maybe. All I know is that every time I think of my grandfather, I now see him in my mind living in abundance, just like I now am. We don't own this house, but have now lived here for 5 years, complete with people who garden, clean, and maintain it. I have my FasterEFT business and Scott has his office here – and he is back doing amazing things, both with investments and charity work. He is definitely in his flow, and wakes up each morning feeling eager to work, purposeful, and happy.

Back to my story. When I was 6 months old, we lived in a country town far from the city. My 2-year-old brother had a life threatening accident. My mother had to leave me with my grandparents (who I hadn't met as they lived in the city) while she went to be at my brother's bedside. Even though my brother had extensive injuries requiring years of physical therapy, I was always jealous of him - yes, it's hard to admit that. In my mind he had my mother's undivided attention. I had to make peace with this too, and forgive myself for my very human jealousy and forgive my mother for 'abandoning me.' As a parent myself I totally understand why she left me, but for the 6-month old still residing in my unconscious, it was a very different story.

FasterEFT allowed me to make peace within myself and, as a result, I have more connected, loving relationships.

Does my mother still favour my brother? Yes. Does it bother me now? Not at all. Am I closer than ever to my mother? Definitely. Do I feel more loving towards my brother? Definitely. I now see him as he is - an awesome man and an amazing testimony of thriving against many odds. FasterEFT allowed me to make peace within myself and, as a result, I have more connected, loving relationships.

My ex-husband and I are now friends.

Although many of my long-term close friends remain true and valued, to this day there were some who judged and rejected us. This hit me hard. The rejection – and my guilt and shame - kept me awake at night. As I cleared memories and tapped on my feelings as they arose, these feelings resolved.

Part of my problem was that years earlier, my first husband had an affair and left me for another woman. They created a new life for themselves, but at the time I felt incredibly heartbroken, bereft and abandoned – and financially stretched, as I was the provider for our children with little extra financial support.

My feelings about the friends left me triggered of all of those earlier feelings, stored in memories of the past, so I had to work on these as well to make peace with the past.

My ex-husband and I are now friends, are very supportive of each other, and he now has a lovely new wife. Making peace with my past reaped so many benefits for me, and, of course, our children.

> I have now attracted into my life new friendships
> which are more open and honest.

With FasterEFT as my tool, I have changed what triggered me unconsciously and presented in the present moment as pain (physical and emotional), fear, anxiety, etc. I have now attracted into my life new friendships which are more open and honest relationships, with people who accept responsibility for themselves without blaming. I now recognise when someone points the finger at you, that three fingers are directed back at themselves! My new friends are awesome – light, fun, connected, accepting. In fact they now reflect who I have become.

My relationship with Scott is better than ever. We are a team! We play together, love, learn, and grow together – and yes also do things independently, individually, and with our own friends.

Scott says he is a much 'better man' now – he is definitely more connected to his heart and more open and kind to others. He also says 'I wasn't smart enough to handle that amount of money.' He is that smart now – both intellectually and emotionally.

Would I wish this experience on anyone? No way!
Have we learnt and grown from it? Definitely.
Do we feel more kind-hearted, loving, connected, stronger, resilient, and emotionally intelligent people? YES!

>If you are willing to make peace with your story,
>you will change what is reflected in your world.

Everyone has a story. Every story is different. You – the reader – have your own story. You have choices. In my practice I see so many people become so attached to their stories. If you are willing to make peace with your story (and yes, yours may be worse than mine), as you change what is held in your mind – often unconsciously – you will change what is reflected in your world. Relationships, health, feelings of worthiness, and finances may all improve. Certainly my joy, love of life, and energy levels have all increased. What is possible for you?

> 'The moment you release your pain, your emotional hurts, your past, you can begin to create a new life and world for yourself.'

In the words of Robert Smith, the Founder of FasterEFT, 'The moment you release your pain, your emotional hurts, your past, you can begin to create a new life and world for yourself.'

Judy Timperon is an experienced Level 4, advanced FasterEFT practitioner. She assists clients to eliminate and manage stress, to achieve health and happiness, and to reach peak performance.

Judy runs workshops and seminars, and mentors other practitioners, bringing a wealth of experience and success to her thriving private practice. She is also part of the FasterEFT Steering Committee and Training Team.

Judy has been a secondary school teacher, adult education teacher, further education lecturer, and curriculum writer – all in health and personal development. She is also a Reiki Master and has completed numerous trainings in other modalities. Her main focus now is FasterEFT, as this is where she has seen the most growth in herself and her clients.

As a FasterEFT practitioner, Judy's work includes addressing: trauma, abuse (physical, sexual, and emotional), fears, phobias, bullying, body pain, anger, anxiety, depression, and addictions. Judy works from her office in Glenelg, South Australia, and also via Skype. You can contact her by email or phone to arrange a session.

Website:
www.findingfreedom.com.au

Email:
judy.timperon@gmail.com

Phone:
(+61) 439990980

My Thoughts Were Responsible for My Weight Issues

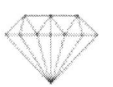

Kim Brown

'Once upon a time. . . ' We all know that's how fairy tales begin.
We all know how they end as well . ' . . . And they lived happily ever after.'

> I felt ugly, stupid, and ashamed - and no one could love me enough to change that.

From an early age I believed this would never be my story. My earliest perceptions were that I was overweight. I felt ugly, stupid, and ashamed - and no one could love me enough to change that. Painful experiences were common in my life, but it was not a life filled with trauma, abandonment, and rejection. I didn't need anyone else to abuse and reject me. I did a fine job on my own.

> Trusting became a guaranteed method of being hurt, and the person I trusted the least was me.

As a young child, I played 'Hide-and-Seek' by hiding right out in the open with my eyes closed. When I was easily discovered by my playmates, I blamed them for cheating. I couldn't see them – so how could they see me? I was naïve, and friends and family enjoyed discovering how long they could continue a ruse with me. Trusting became a guaranteed method of being hurt, and the person I trusted the least was me.

Even God didn't notice me.

I grew up and lived my life, but in my eyes, everyone else in the world was enjoying life, living, loving, and laughing – AND they were completely oblivious to me and my pain! Why didn't they notice? I was convinced that even God didn't notice me. I had prayed for my heart's desire for years and years, and that prayer was never answered. My family loved me, I had six precious children who loved me, but they were not enough. And yes, that caused my children emotional pain as well.

I stopped listening to any form of music, especially if it praised God. Hearing about the blessings others received or the goodness of a loving God when I was so hopeless was more than I could bear. I did believe God was good. So, the only thing that made sense was that I must have done something unforgivable at such an early age that I could no longer remember it.

Fear controlled me
and I considered it part of my family heritage.

Fear controlled me and I considered it part of my family heritage. My father was an interesting combination of courage and fear, and the apple didn't fall far from the tree. I didn't pursue the course of study I preferred in college because of fear. After I got engaged, I was afraid I wouldn't live long enough to get married. Then, I was afraid I would never have children. Even when I was pregnant, I was afraid I wouldn't live long enough to give birth or that the baby would die before it was born. After my children were born, I was afraid for them to be out of my care and supervision.

Even though my husband had a good job and made a comfortable salary, we lived from paycheck to paycheck. The belief that we didn't have enough permeated every area of our lives. We drove broken down cars and wore hand-me-downs. There was never enough, so why bother planning, budgeting, or saving.

My body found ways to let me know how uncomfortable I was in my own skin. For instance, I had been allergic to watermelon and cats since childhood. Later in life, I developed painful bursitis, which was at its worst when I was a busy wife and mother in my 30s. Wasn't it quite fitting to have an auto immune disease? It made perfect sense for my body to attack itself when I was so afraid all the time.

I felt deprived of my deepest need – to be noticed and loved for who I was - so there was no way I was going to be deprived of food, too.

I had to soothe myself, of course. Caffeinated sodas and chocolate became my dearest friends. I overate. I ate even when I wasn't hungry. I felt deprived of my deepest need – to be noticed and loved for who I was - so there was no way I was going to be deprived of food, too.

A good friend found FasterEFT on YouTube while searching for relief from a serious illness. He experienced some benefits, but thought it might be wishful thinking. He asked if he could test it out and practice on me with weight loss. I agreed, not because I had any hope - that was all gone. I agreed because I felt safe with my friend and wanted to help him in his studies. He mentioned that FasterEFT could also help with my emotional pain, but I refused. I told him we could work on the weight, but nothing else.

I began to realize that my thoughts were responsible for my weight issues as well as my emotional pain!

Imagine my surprise when I began to realize that my thoughts were responsible for my weight issues as well as my emotional pain! I was even more surprised that I actually had the ability to remove the destructive painful thoughts and replace them with healthy positive ones.

I can now not only love and value the people in my world but receive their love as well.

Consistently working with my practitioner friend for the next 6 months, I lost 50 pounds. While that was my goal and I am thankful, the inner transformation has been the most amazing. I love and value myself. As a result, I can now not only love and value the people in my world but receive their love as well. And yes, my children have experienced that emotional freedom as well. I can't control the circumstances in my world, but thanks to FasterEFT, I can control my responses to them.

I no longer fear death. I was with my mother as she took her final breath, and the experience was a beautiful blessing for me. I am no longer terrified to fly. I've flown many times over the last few years, even flying to New Zealand. I am no longer hiding out in the open. I am a full time FasterEFT practitioner, making FasterEFT informational and instructive videos, speaking at events, and facilitating sessions with clients.

I no longer overeat.

I am living abundantly and the freedom is indescribable.

I'm no longer allergic to cats. I've spent several nights with my daughter, who has an indoor cat, and I experienced no allergic reactions. I'm no longer allergic to watermelon. I no longer overeat. I'm no longer addicted to sodas and chocolate. Money no longer intimidates me. I bought my college-bound daughter a car with cash as well as furnished her apartment. I tithe, I donate, and I invest. I no longer feel deprived and without. I am no longer controlled by fear. I am capable. I am confident. I see the blessings of my life and I enjoy them. I am living abundantly and the freedom is indescribable.

I am living happily ever after!

Now with perfect confidence I know that God loves me and has a beautiful plan for my life. And I am living it! My story has changed, and I am living happily ever after!

TODAY is a new day!

No matter what you've experienced in the past, TODAY is a new day!

Kim Brown is a mom of six, a wife, sister, community volunteer, and FasterEFT practitioner who lives in Florida in the United States. She has helped people around the world by teaching them to apply the life-changing techniques of FasterEFT.

Using FasterEFT, Kim lost 50 pounds in 6 months and has kept it off for 5 years. While that has been wonderful, she believes the most amazing transformation has been losing the weight of emotional pain she carried for so many years. Now she's free to love herself and her life, and she's confident to pursue her interests and finally be successful at something besides misery. She has had her life totally transformed using FasterEFT and has witnessed the transformation in her clients worldwide.

Website:

www.KimBrown.Today

Email:

kimbrowntoday@gmail.com

FaceBook: https://www.facebook.com/KimBrownToday/

YouTube:

https://www.youtube.com/channel/UC9xvRahqE3B_1pe0fOhM8hg

: can you Believe it !

From Stressed to Success

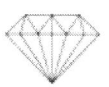

Kim Jewell

It was late 2010 . . . . My ex-husband had left six months earlier, and I had decided to go back to work full time after months of trying, to no avail, to make ends meet financially. I had not worked full time in over twenty years. I struggled with the thought of having to be in a job every day, with the stress, the expectations, and the constant self-doubt.

I was 24 years sober.
My anxiety was back and peaking like never before.

I was 24 years sober. My anxiety was back and peaking like never before. Years of working a twelve-step program had helped me know I couldn't pick up a drink - but didn't do anything to help the unbearable insecurity that plagued my thoughts constantly. Nights were the worst. I was unable to sleep because my mind raced relentlessly, and I dreaded mornings and what they might bring.

Why could everyone else get it together and have great lives?
All I ever wanted was to be normal

Why could everyone else get it together and have great lives? Yet for me, every day was just another harrowing experience of trying to hold it together and trying to appear normal. All I could think was, 'What's wrong with me? What am I doing wrong?' All I ever wanted was to be normal - to be free to live without the constant state of stress.

This wasn't an unfamiliar state of being for me, because I have felt like this since the first grade. It just never seemed to go away. Now, at almost fifty-one years of age, divorced, and with three teenage children depending on me, I felt almost as bad as I had when I first walked through the door of the 12-step program all those year ago. All I wanted was freedom from the excruciating inner criticism, self-doubt, judgment, and FEAR that seemed to dominate my world.

On the outside, it looked like I had everything - the house, the job, three beautiful children, and the husband. Except now he was gone, and on the inside I still felt the pressing question: 'How am I going to survive?'

I got a job as a drug and alcohol counselor, and it was rewarding; but my employers had asked me to go back to school and get a degree in psychology. I secretly didn't think I could do it. School had always been a nightmare for me, and working for years with psychologists and psychiatrists had not increased my confidence in traditional counseling methods. I didn't really believe they were effective, and they certainly hadn't helped me.

I made the decision to study an alternative method of helping others. I had already completed one alternative modality that I had seen help so many people before returning to full time work. I loved working with it, but it felt too far left of mainstream for most people. It was very spiritually based, and my employers would not let me use it at work. The truth was, it helped me become more centered but had not helped me get the freedom I had been searching for all these years.

I set out to learn neurolinguistic programming (NLP), as it seemed to be the common denominator of all the other emotional healing modalities I'd heard of up to that point. By early 2011, I had become a Master Practitioner of NLP and was studying to become a trainer.

But anxiety continued to be a major factor in my life. The NLP had helped to alleviate it, but it was still strong. And my self-doubt, while improving, still played a major factor in my every decision. I wasn't convinced that the NLP would be enough and had started thinking maybe I should add another modality to the work I did to help myself.

It was when I was due to go to Sydney to take my final exam as an NLP Trainer - and my nerves and anxiety were through the roof - that I decided I should watch someone else working with NLP to make sure I was doing it right. I went to my computer, did some searches in YouTube, and what came up was a video by Robert G. Smith.

I sat mesmerized by what Robert was doing on the video. A part of me was aware that this man, this guy from Oklahoma, had put together what I had been searching for, studying, and trying to work out for the past 24 years. As I watched, I could see what he was doing (because of the training I'd already had), and I understood instantly why it was working. I sat at my computer with mixed emotions - excitement, hope, disbelief, jealousy, and confusion! I called out to a friend who was also studying NLP to come and watch. Then I proceeded to sit and watch YouTube videos by Robert for the next three days. I searched Google to see if he was doing any training here in Australia. As it turned out, he was coming out in a few short months, and my excitement was uncontainable!

I went to that first training feeling hopeful, and I left knowing that my life would never be the same.

I went to that first training feeling hopeful, and I left knowing that my life would never be the same. No, I didn't have one of those amazing moments of transformation. I sat through the training, watching people get worked on, and seeing their changes happening. In the end, I couldn't get up to sit in Robert's 'magic' demonstration chair and have him work with me one-on-one in front of the group. I so wanted to, but I just couldn't talk about my stuff in front of everyone.

Two hours after my session, I walked out thinking and feeling that nothing much had happened.

Robert was also giving private sessions, and my friend convinced me to book one. Two hours after my session, I walked out thinking and feeling that nothing much had happened and that I could do the same thing with what I learned in NLP. Robert was very relaxed and down to earth. We worked on memories of sexual abuse and my drinking. At one point I remember him picking up a glass with ice and shaking it. Out of nowhere I could taste the alcohol going down my throat as if it were happening now!

Those were the only two things that I remembered that we worked on, yet I knew I had gone in with a very long list. I didn't really feel that much different at first. I started to feel a little skeptical, but I remember telling my friend that only time would tell.

'Have you noticed how calm you are about the test?'

Fast-forward two months. It was time to take the NLP Trainers test, and I flew to Sydney with my friend. It was on the bus that she started to point out a few differences. She said, 'Look at your feet - your toes!' At first I wasn't sure what she meant. Then I looked down as she said, 'We could go and get a pedicure!' And then she asked me, 'Have you noticed how calm you are about the test?' It was then that I realized some changes had taken place after all.

You see, from the time I was a little girl, I used to rip my toenails off as a by-product of my anxiety. I did it so often that I had stopped being aware that I did it. I could never get a pedicure because I never had toenails. As I looked down and saw how long my toenails were, it started to dawn on me that my head wasn't racing the way it normally did, and we were on our way to take a test - and I wasn't even worried. I went through the exam period completely relaxed and confident.

> I was able to interact for the first time in 40 years with the person I had blamed for so long.

The sexual abuse memory not only dissipated but became just a story, and I was able to see that this experience had helped to mold me into the incredible healer that I am today. Not only that, I was able to interact for the first time in 40 years with the person I had blamed for so long. Not only able to forgive and interact - but now to have an amazing friendship with that person. In such a short time, my life started to become comfortable.

That was just the beginning. Things started to change at a rapid rate, and I was sold on FasterEFT and how it had changed my life. I couldn't get enough. I knew I wanted to be a part of such an amazing modality and that I wanted to share it with the world.

After that first training I have never looked back. I am grateful for my persistence, for FasterEFT, for Robert G. Smith, and for every practitioner that has helped me release the baggage along the way.

I am now a Master Level 4 FasterEFT Practitioner. My life is unrecognizable from 5 years ago. I have written a book, *From Stress to Success*, to help others see just how simple it is to change their lives. I have a full time practice helping people facilitate those changes. I also speak internationally and deliver personal development seminars all around the world.

can you Believe it !

I am fortunate enough to give back twice a year by volunteering at **_Habilitat, Inc._**, a long term substance abuse center where myself and ten other practitioners volunteer, helping addicts release the emotional drivers that keep them trapped in addiction.

> FasterEFT gave me the vehicle to set myself free
> and show others how they, too, can be free.

At that first personal development seminar all those years ago, I realized that I wanted to be a light for others who have suffered like me. FasterEFT gave me the vehicle to set myself free and show others how they, too, can be free.

I am addiction-free, I am anxiety-free, I have a quiet mind, and I love my life today! I am happy, joyous, and FREE!

Kim Jewell is a life coach who lives in Queensland, Australia. She has studied a number of healing modalities and has several qualifications, including Master NLP practitioner and trainer, certified hypnotherapist, and Level 4 Master FasterEFT practitioner. She is the owner and founder of Inner Stillness Integrative Wellness Practice in Brisbane.

Kim has a full-time practice helping people to make meaningful changes in their lives. She works with clients in her office or via Skype. In addition, she travels internationally to speak and give seminars on a regular basis.

Websites:

www.KimJewell.com.au

www.fastereft.net.au

Email:

info@fastereft.net.au

Telephone:

(+61) 418 642 021

Link to Kim's Book:

https://www.amazon.com/Stress-Success-Emotionally-Focused-Transformations-ebook/dp/B00AA85YSU.

I Don't Need to be Invisible Anymore

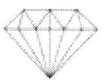

Dr. Linda Wilson

Before I came across FasterEFT I was a practicing doctor of Traditional Chinese Medicine (TCM). I had taken a break from my practice to raise my children with the view that I was interested in looking at expanding my skills and potentially branching out.

FasterEFT has given me my biggest breakthroughs, insights, and experiences of myself and my life and continues to do so.

When I was asked to contribute to this book I was delighted. I sat down to write my story and found it difficult to start. One of the truly wonderful things about FasterEFT is that when you do the work, it is actually hard to remember how things used to be. You are changed at a cellular level, and going 'backwards' just seems boring. So my story is more of a meander through my learnings and how they have influenced the direction of my life and continue to do so.

TINY TRAUMAS

I have no doubt that there will be stories in this book from people who have recovered from extreme trauma in their lives. I am in admiration, and I send them my deepest love and respect.

> A slow erosion where I believed in
> my own powerlessness and unlovability.

My story is not like that. In comparison you could describe my life and the hardships I have experienced as just a series of mini and often mundane traumas across time, a slow erosion of confidence and the accumulation of experiences where I believed in my own powerlessness and unlovability. But that is not how it felt as an emotionally sensitive and energetically wide-open child. I know that the 'tiny traumas' experience is a common one for many.

Using traditional forms of talk therapy can make us the 'hardest' clients because we have nothing definitive to focus on. The 'mini trauma' concept from FasterEFT was a relief to me. I discovered I actually had a right to be hurt by my experiences even when they might appear trivial to others. It is all about interpretation. Whilst my quiet revelations about my life through the use of FasterEFT might not compare to others, they rocked my deeply sensitive world and therefore by extension the world of those around me. They continue to do so in the connection and efficacy of my life and my work, and I am so deeply grateful. I also believe when my clients know I can relate to their lives of quiet desperation, they relax. So many of them come to me feeling almost guilty for not being happy. Their external world is working well, and they have no 'big Ts' to talk about. The permissiveness and forgiveness inherent in the FasterEFT process allows all to feel they have a right to their feelings and when they are ready, a right to let them go.

> The 'importance' is based on how strongly we feel about it.

Not knowing how to express my multiple 'tiny Ts' as a definitive experience, but learning I just had to be aware of my 'felt' experience of them, is the great leveler in FasterEFT. We can all do this without going into judgement about the relative value or importance of any given event in relation to the experiences of anyone else. The 'importance' is based on how strongly we feel about it. This cannot be argued with. It simply is.

Being Broken

One of the most transformational things I learnt from Robert G. Smith was that there are no broken people; you are perfectly producing what you hold within you. If you don't like what you are producing you are simply operating from outdated belief systems or rules that are no longer serving you.

> If I was not broken and simply producing what I know and doing it really well, wasn't I actually a success?

This was incredibly profound for me and was the true beginning of my breakthroughs with FasterEFT. If I was not broken and simply producing what I know and doing it really well, wasn't I actually a success? I had spent so much time feeling a failure that this literally rocked my world. I remember sitting unable to speak and wondering how the world continued to turn on its axis, as this concept exploded my consciousness. I felt my entire psyche transform, my body shift, and at my core knew things would never be the same. It was a real *When Harry Met Sally* 'I want what she's having' moment. This was just the first of my profound experiences. Since then there have been many more. I also hope there will continue to be even more as life happens and I commit to knowing myself more deeply.

All we have to do is change what we hold within us - and we will perfectly produce that.

The wonderful realization this concept gave me was that if I *changed* the rules or feelings about the things I held inside of myself that I thought were true, if I uncovered my unconscious belief systems and dismantled them, I would be capable of something else. If we are not broken and are simply perfectly producing what we hold within us, then all we have to do is change what we hold within us - and we will perfectly produce that.

I found this concept deeply, deeply moving. I could finally forgive myself. I am not broken. Neither are you.
It was these physical, emotional, intellectual, and spiritually 'felt' experiences that I had with FasterEFT - and that I had never achieved with any other modality - that inspire me each and every day.

I just didn't know how to relate to others and therefore to me. I had no language for it and no voice.

Setting Up Beliefs

I grew up in the center of Australia. In those days Alice Springs was a very small town in the middle of the desert, hundreds of miles from the next small town, and thousands of miles to the city. I lived in a street of boys where I was the tag-along little sister. I was viewed as an irritation, a pain, and someone to be ignored. I could only join in if I could physically keep up. The only reason this is relevant is because the isolation of the environment and my difference from those around me might give you an indication of the disconnection and isolation I felt as soon as I became aware. I just didn't know how to relate to others and therefore to me. I had no language for it and no voice. Becoming 'invisible' was a smart move. As we do, I thought this was normal even though it didn't feel good. And, as we tend to do, I blamed myself.

Back then it was OK to belt your kids and use verbal aggression and the threat of violence to keep them in line.

Interpretation

My parents loved us, but they were in a world of personal relationship pain and didn't have the skills to focus on our emotional wellbeing. They did the best they could, and it was a pretty good job; however, my up-bringing made it all too easy to ascribe negative feelings and situations to the responsibility of someone else. Blame was big. There was (what was interpreted by me) a constant sense of 'threat' and deeply unhappy people in my home. The sense that at any moment my Dad could be triggered into aggression or violence, or that my parents could have another argument, or that we would get into trouble and get 'the strap' meant treading on eggshells and trying to be a 'good girl' or, even better, invisible. Back then it was OK to belt your kids and use verbal aggression and the threat of violence to keep them in line. That, or coldness and disapproval.

Forgiveness

My internalization of disapproval, coldness, and the harsh and violent way I criticized and dealt with myself was something I struggled with for many years as I co-opted the 'story of my parents' into my own judgement of self. That is, until FasterEFT allowed me to forgive myself for not being 'enough' - enough to solve my parents' unhappiness, enough to calm my father or win the approval of my mother, enough to trust I was lovable, and enough to be a child instead of a hypervigilant and lonely adult in a child's body.

FasterEFT taught me that my parents both deeply loved me the best way they possibly could, that I was prized and treasured exactly the way I dreamed of, and that they grieved their responses and reactions when they had the capacity to assess them. This is a gift beyond measure. It did not happen easily. I had to work at it. It is only now, and in each and every day that I use FasterEFT, that I no longer have this as a reference for who I am or actually who I ever was.

Grief and Reconnection

Another profound experience I am so grateful to FasterEFT for was during the time I lost both my father and a treasured aunt. These deaths happened in quick succession. After their passing, people were confused and even worried that I was so matter of fact. My peacefulness alarmed them as they felt I should be in some way suffering from such losses. I did suffer. For 24 hours after each of their deaths. During the 24 hours I tapped continually. I rewrote my history with my father until I remembered the precious memories of his love for me that I had forgotten. I gave myself and my father the love that had been missing because prior to that our relationship was one of conflict and hurt. All I could feel was the regret.

That 24 hours of continuous tapping was the greatest gift I could have given myself and the greatest respect I could have shown my father. I now love him with compassion, with respect, and with great joy. I feel connected to him in a way I never could when he was alive, although I had made much peace with him before he passed.

In regards to my aunt, peacefulness was so much easier to find because although she was like a parent to me, and an enormous and loving influence in my life, I was grateful that she was not suffering. I could let her go because I loved her enough to do so. FasterEFT means it's hard to be selfish, and you can choose to be incredibly generous. Both of these people are with me in my life just as much now as when they were alive.

My children are clear where I end and they begin.

Parenting

As an avid tapper, I have managed to go back and rewrite the way I had parented, as well. My children are clear where I end and they begin. They are their own people, entirely capable of calling me on my stuff should it show up. They are not just a product of others but deeply, intrinsically, and wonderfully themselves. I have been able to forgive my less-than-perfect mothering, recognizing that when I knew better I did better. I am fiercely proud of my children and their ability to recognize and master their own emotions.

Blame is not a 'go to' emotion, and responsibility is a constant conversation. Apparently my love and open pride in them is 'embarrassing.' How wonderful. I also know that my children will always have ways in which I am their problem. This may be the way they distinguish themselves from me as their parent. I am happy to be wrong, and it is their right to protest. This is a dramatic shift from how parenting was modeled to me.

Purpose and Vision

FasterEFT has helped me to recognize my purpose in life and to develop and express my vision of that purpose. My purpose is to empower every person I connect with by providing tools to transform that which no longer serves them and to put self-care and self-management front and centre in every life. Where I felt I had no language and no voice, I now provide opportunities for others to express themselves on my radio show, mentor a team of practitioners to be their best selves and achieve their goals, and take my skills into corporations where I can influence thousands. I write books, am a regular blog contributor, have an online course, and am a leader in my field. I touch the individual lives of my one-on-one clients in a way that is an honour and a privilege.

This is just the beginning of my vision.

I was my feelings rather than simply experiencing them

Consciousness and Connection

FasterEFT has allowed me a level of self-awareness and consciousness that previously eluded me. I was my feelings rather than simply experiencing them. The freedom in this is enormous. You can take yourself on in a really powerful way. I mean, you can still sulk if you want to but it gets old very, very quickly. Before FasterEFT I could disappear for weeks into a spiral of 'victim' thinking. It just doesn't happen anymore, and, if it does ever creep in, I am so much more aware of my own thoughts that I catch it almost instantly.

When you use FasterEFT, you are aware of possibility all around you. Every event or experience that upsets, triggers, or worries you is an opportunity to clean out some more of your junk! It is liberating because I don't know of anything else that allows you to do that for yourself in the moment that is also capable of changing your neuro-chemistry and physiology around the issue for good!

> I can focus on a solution instead of feeling the story.

Cold Compassion

When you can be aware of yourself, you also develop a capacity to be far more compassionate and less judgmental of others. This has been described as 'cold compassion.' It is an apt description of being able to view, hear, and support another person out of their painful stories and not have it become your own. It means I can focus on a solution instead of feeling the story. At the same time as I can have great empathy for another's experience, it does not become my own.

I don't need to be invisible any more.

One of the things I have heard time and time again from clients who are your more traditional 'talk therapists' is that after a while the stories become overwhelming. They have no way to debrief that is as powerful as tapping. Luckily for me, 98 percent of the time I do not think about my clients outside of the room. All the pain, etc, is dismantled within the room and it is done. As a practitioner, this is such a blessing. Oh, and the 2 percent? That's work for me to do on myself.

Do I still have dark days? Yes, because life happens. Does it take me down? Sometimes momentarily, but I am more resilient, confidant, and sure of myself and my value and ability than I have ever been. I cannot imagine what life would be like without finding and implementing FasterEFT.

FasterEFT has also allowed me to be vulnerable and honest about my feelings and not feel as though I will be destroyed if I reveal them. It makes me stronger. I don't need to be invisible any more. I am so proud to help bring this tool to my world.

Dr Linda Wilson is the author of STRESS MADE EASY – PEELING WOMEN OFF THE CEILING. *She consults and owns a multi-modality wellness practice and has an online program designed to assist women to reclaim themselves when 'life happens.' As well as seeing clients one-on-one, Linda is a corporate wellness consultant running tailored programs on stress management which incorporate the latest neurological research, tools, and techniques to create sustainable stress management plans and behaviours.*

Linda has her own weekly radio show which focuses on health and wellness for business and individuals. She is often asked to be a guest on podcasts, webinars, online forums and to speak or present because of her unique take on how taking personal responsibility for changing your mind will change your world.

Informed by the philosophy of a degree in Traditional Chinese Medicine, a Graduate Diploma in Education (Health), and 17 years of clinical experience, Linda has helped thousands of clients better Identify, understand, and manage themselves and their contribution to the world.

Website:

www.drlindawilson.com

I Help People Feel Good... It's That Simple!

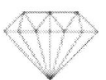

Linda Ledwidge

Welcome and congratulations on making the choice to be healthy and happy!

You have found your way to this book because you are looking for something. You may or may not know exactly what that is, however you don't really have to know. Very often the answers lie in what we do not know. Let me tell you a little bit about myself and explain why I am passionate about helping people feel good.

> At no time in any of my training were we encouraged to look at the mind/body connection.

My background is in conventional medicine. I trained as a general nurse in Glasgow, and then as a midwife. I have been interested in all modalities of healing and the mind/body connection since I can remember - and I always felt that there was more to helping people to heal than I had been trained to do. My whole medical training was based on symptom relief. At no time in any of my training were we encouraged to look at the mind/body connection. The whole medical establishment breaks everything down into areas. Psychology deals with emotional issues. Then you have medical problems, which are symptoms of illness in the body and the use of drugs to relieve these symptoms. Then there is surgery. Well if it can be cut out, then problem solved . . . no?

Medicine has evolved from looking at the person as a whole to specializing in the different body systems.

Medicine has evolved from looking at the person as a whole to specializing in the different body systems. We have specialists in cardiovascular, renal, neurological, and other diseases. In my opinion this has made it even more challenging in the treatment of disease. How can we heal someone if we only investigate and treat one area - when we are WHOLE PERSONS and not just separate 'ill parts'?

As happens, I got sidetracked with my daily life. I married, had children, worked, and put all my energy into my family life. I forgot that I had wanted at one time to pursue my interest in health therapies.

I was told everywhere I turned
that this was an incurable disease

In 2004 I was diagnosed with Trigeminal Neuralgia (TN), and, for the next 6 years, I spent my life in a drugged haze. TN, a disorder of the trigeminal nerve, is considered to be one of the most painful afflictions known to medicine. Can you imagine suffering from a disease no one can see and which causes such excruciating pain? In fact, TN has been nicknamed 'the suicide disease.' I was told everywhere I turned that this was an incurable disease, and that, at best, we could hope to control the pain – but that I would simply have to 'live with it.'

I underwent a range of scans, was prescribed various drugs, and had injections into my face. I even had major surgery, called Microvascular decompression (MVD), in which the neurosurgeon inserted Gortex between the compressing vessel and the nerve. The surgery gave about 7 weeks relief before the pain returned with a vengeance. I spent many days in hospital as only intravenous drugs could help in any way to dull the pain. In November 2007, my neurosurgeon told me that there was no other treatment that he could try. Nothing seemed to be working.

This was my life. My only hope was to find some way of controlling the pain - so my surgeon referred me to another doctor, a neurologist, who would try further concoctions of drug therapy.

Being a stubborn Scot, I refused to accept this and started my search for a cure. I had looked at and tried some complimentary therapies, however I was still very much a conventional medicine kind of person because, after all, it was my training!

In January 2008, a few days after leaving hospital again, I was feeling particularly low, and my husband had a meeting with a client who was also a friend of ours. He asked me to go along to get me out of the house, and, after a lot of cajoling, I agreed. Susan, a friend who had also come along that day, then spoke some words that would become a turning point in my life. Very hesitatingly, she said, 'Linda, I know that this may sound a bit strange, and please feel free to ignore me, however I have had some treatment from a man in the UK who is a Spiritual Healer - and he has managed to help me. If you would like, I will give you his contact details.' Well I was at the stage where I was ready to try anything.

By now I realized that, as far as the doctors were concerned, there was no cure for this condition. The thought that I was facing a life of drug therapy and hospitalization was more than I could bear. I made an appointment to see Ray Brown on the 5th March 2008, and that step changed my life, forever.

'I believe that anything can be healed. I believe this because I am living proof'.

I am not sure what shifted that day. All I know is that I am so grateful that none of the conventional treatments helped to control this condition because, if they had, it might have taken me even longer to discover how miraculous and wonderful our bodies are.

'I believe that anything can be healed. I believe this because I am living proof'.

This one step opened the door for me into the world of (w)holistic healing. I started to look into and seriously study different therapies. My sessions with Ray were the start. After seeing him, the TN was becoming controllable. I was still taking drugs, although not as often - and I was not being lifted from the floor, writhing in pain, and taken to hospital every week. For obvious reasons my long-dormant interest in complimentary therapies was reawakened. I spent time studying with Ray Brown in Granada in 2009 and then went on to study and train in naturopathy, nutritional therapy, hypnosis, and FasterEFT. After three appointments with Ray, and two years of self-healing, I finally became drug-free and pain-free. I have been healthy since.

Research on the internet led me to Robert's videos on YouTube, and the resonance that I felt with FasterEFT encouraged me to go to a level 1 training in Deal, England. Over time, through continuing training, I have become an advanced FasterEFT practitioner, gaining my Level 4 certification while volunteering at the Habilitat drug rehabilitation centre in Hawaii.

FasterEFT has changed my life in unimaginable ways.

FasterEFT has changed my life in unimaginable ways.
I have learned that mind and body interact and mutually influence each other. It is not possible to make a change in one without the other being affected. When we think differently, our bodies change. When we act differently, we change our thoughts and feelings.

FasterEFT is a way of life. The FasterEFT belief system is easy to understand and logical . . . . We believe that there are no broken people. We are all operating successfully based on our own internal belief system. Your belief system is built from your past experiences, which are all filed away in your subconscious.

> 'Our body has its own innate intelligence for self-healing. I can show you how to get out of the way and allow it.'

Inspired to use my knowledge and experience to help others I use the **KISS** – *keep it super simple* - approach to self-healing. I invite you to join me and others in learning and using this approach to help you to be happier, healthier and enjoy the most joyous life.

'Our body has its own innate intelligence for self-healing. I can show you how to get out of the way and allow it.'

Linda is a holistic health practitioner who is also a qualified general nurse, midwife, and naturopath. She has studied and become certified in several holistic healing modalities, including hypnosis, and is a Level 4 FasterEFT practitioner. Originally from Scotland, she now lives in Mallorca, Spain, and works with people all over the world to help them discover the way to a healthy, happy life.

*Linda's **KISS** approach to self-healing (keep it super simple!) has helped many others to achieve what they desire in their life using logical, simple tools to balance and maintain health and happiness.*

Linda believes that we all have the divine right to live a happy, healthy, and joyous life. Her passion is to show you how to make that choice!

Website:

www.lindaledwidge.com

can you Believe it !

Email:

linda@lindaledwidge.com

Mobile:

+34 692062290

Skype:

linda9166

My Journey to Serenity, Healing and Balance

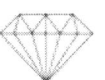

Margherita Harrington

From an early age, I felt I was a square peg in a round hole. And so many times, I felt that I was a disappointment, both to myself and to others.

I remember feeling as a child that I was too outspoken. I think my parents expected me to be easily obedient, but I had something to say even at an early age. Also, I wanted to draw, paint, read, and dance – while my parents (especially my father) had different expectations. My dad hadn't followed his family's musical vocation, yet pressed me to become a pianist when I didn't have the full interest or talent for it.

I did study piano for several years and eventually grew to love playing, but I think most everyone realized after a while that I would never have the ability to be a musical professional.

Meanwhile, I began experiencing illnesses from about age 5, when I had a kidney infection and had to be hospitalized. A few years later I had Salmonella. In my teens I suffered pneumonia and then intestinal problems. I was relieved when my health stabilized during my college years.

Two weeks before my college graduation, my family was thrown into upheaval and sadness when my father died. Fortunately, I was hired for full-time work soon after graduation, so I was not at loose ends physically or mentally. After a year of secretarial work I began my career in publishing - working my way up to editing and publications management. As for my personal pursuits, in my early 20s I began studying dance as much as I could - ballet, tap, ballroom, modern, and folk – so I was feeling fulfilled.

As times passed, my work became more stressful. I had loved school as a child, but sometimes I was bullied, starting in elementary school. Now as an adult, in addition to the standard stresses many people experience at work, I sometimes was also harassed. Why was I being singled out again?

I started to expect negative experiences.

I couldn't figure out how to manage all these stresses and felt an inertia about finding a new job. By now in my early thirties, new illnesses started to surface. I developed asthma and had foot surgery. I started to expect negative experiences. My father's death right before my college graduation had given me a fear of looking forward to something. Why get your hopes up only to be devastated later? Then one day I fell while running to catch a subway train and got some painful injuries. Within a few months I was constantly tired. After really struggling to live with the fatigue and then becoming nearly incapacitated, I was diagnosed with chronic fatigue syndrome (CFS).

I was now used to being ill and started
accepting that state as my identity.

---

can you Believe it !

I was now used to being ill and started accepting that state as my identity. My 'new normal,' if I could get out of bed at all, was to avoid many activities, ration my energy, and define myself by illness. After several months, I recovered enough to work full-time again, and life started going back to a good place. I got married and became a stepmother. But some lingering issues flared up, and, after a 20-year career, had to leave my job. Then, just as I was just getting used to my new life and regaining my strength, my mother's home was broken into and vandalized one evening while I was visiting. The stress of the event, including the court case, affected many aspects of my life. Soon, I had a new illness. I didn't know it at first, but the large itchy rash I had in August of 2005 was from a tick bite. I now had Lyme disease.

I felt powerless

After getting Lyme, I researched both the illness and healing protocols, which helped me feel I had some control. I learned a lot - but I also began to dwell on being sick, letting fear get the best of me at times. Doctor after doctor had told me I shouldn't be feeling ill after 3 weeks of antibiotic treatment. As with CFS, I felt powerless and relied on the advice of support groups and others who had the same illness. I started exploring the mind/body connection that other Lyme patients were saying was part of the healing process. I had previously bought Louise Hay's book *You Can Heal Your Life*. The colorful drawings, encouraging words, and lists of physical manifestations for emotional concerns had always appealed to me, especially when I felt at my worst.

> I was realizing
> how strongly the mind could influence the body.

Soon, I was realizing how strongly the mind could influence the body. Living with CFS taught me to be gentle with myself and feel gratitude. Now living with Lyme was teaching me to proactively work on healing.

I continued to try out and study many approaches to health. Little by little since leaving my job, I was completing classes in biology, herbology, homeopathy, and even chemistry by distance learning. I did some mainstream and then holistic treatments for Lyme, and they helped me improve quite a bit. But Lyme had brought on additional issues. I now had food sensitivities, and I couldn't take certain antibiotics anymore. I had to have my gallbladder removed, and developed a hernia from that surgery - so then another surgery was required. I grew tired of spending so much time and money on doctors, medical tests, medicines, and supplements.

> I started to have hope that there was more out there for me
> than a prescription, an intravenous drip,
> or a cabinet full of supplements.

While enrolled in a holistic treatment program for people with CFS and fibromyalgia, I was taught to use a few different energy healing modalities. Although none of those methods really resonated with me, I started to have hope that there was more out there for me than a prescription, an intravenous drip, or a cabinet full of supplements. I started to hope that I could rely on something inside myself, and I kept exploring and learning alternative healing methods.

One day, while feeling extra tired and stressed, I asked my chiropractor if he had any recommendations for effective healing modalities. He told me that one of his patients had been doing very poorly and now was so much better. He sent me her number, and soon I was booked for a FasterEFT session with the wonderful Heather McKean. She kindly drove nearly an hour to meet at my house since I was too fatigued to go to her.

Right from the beginning, I experienced some amazing changes with FasterEFT! I started to feel physically better, emotionally more relaxed, and also began to release long-held fears and resentments. I soon even released the need to automatically blame circumstances and people. When something upsetting came up or a past event began to bother me, I tapped on myself then and there - in the moment - to release the problem. And I was gaining so much energy! After about four sessions, Heather told me she thought I should go to FasterEFT training. I was shocked! How could I become a practitioner and help others? Didn't I need to take it easy? Look at everything that had been wrong with me over the years!

In the meantime, my husband broke his leg, and I thought that this would be my way out. 'I won't have to go to training now!' came up in the recesses of my brain. I could just keep living my comfortable (yet limited) life. But instead of cancelling my upcoming session with Heather, something made me keep it. During that session, she helped me see that my husband's leg was almost healed, and that going to Level 1 training would help me. And, of course, she was right.

From the very first day of the Level 1 seminar in February 2014, I knew I was with others who were committed to healing and moving forward in a positive way. Here were people who had experienced difficult situations too. I was so impressed by my classmates. I was so impressed by Robert G Smith (the originator of FasterEFT), Deirdre Maguire (Master Practitioner and trainer who was so motivating and caring), and all the other advanced practitioners in attendance who were there to support new FasterEFT students. Watching Robert help people change their perceptions within the space of 45 minutes was inspiring. As the week progressed, I made friends and gained more confidence. A few months later, I went back for my Level 2 certification.

The autumn after my Level 2 training, I took a break from FasterEFT training to concentrate on a challenging class for my master's program in Natural Health. During the semester, what I thought was a 'minor' car accident brought whiplash and other lingering injuries. But this year, I'm finally going to my Level 3 training! With the help of some wonderful healers (chiropractors, acupuncturists, and physical therapists) AND my FasterEFT family (practitioners and swapping partners), I'm feeling much better. I had lingering dizziness form the accident, so my balance is still a work in progress – but that is both physical and emotional. I know that this physical issue has come up because I needed to improve how I 'balance' aspects of my life.

Sometimes things happen we don't like. FasterEFT helps us to deal with those events and to be much more proactive at making corrections where they're needed.

Life has changed for the better for me because I've changed. It's so much easier to avoid excuses and stop blaming others. If something stressful happens, and even if I'm unkind to myself, I can soon recognize it, tap on it, and move on.

I'm so enjoying this amazing journey
to become my best self!!!

I look forward to continuing to make great changes in my life. I'm so enjoying this amazing journey to become my best self!!!

Margherita Harrington is a stress-relief coach and FasterEFT practitioner. Since leaving full-time work due to CFS and fibromyalgia several years ago, she has taken numerous science and natural health courses, and has studied and used various energetic and emotional healing modalities. She continues to work toward higher-level FasterEFT skills and certifications.

Ever since experiencing the benefits of FasterEFT, Margherita has improved her health and personal serenity - as well as increased her accomplishments in every aspect of life. She recently launched her new practitioner website called 'Your Journey to You: Transform and Enjoy Your Life.' Her company name is based on her view that we can navigate life's journey with better outcomes if we do the right things for ourselves.

Margherita also does freelance editing and publishing work, and she has started an additional business with her husband. She believes none of these productive and fulfilling changes would have happened if not for FasterEFT.

Margherita lives in her home state of Virginia, in the United States. She enjoys traveling and making new friends from across the world.

Website:

www.YourJourneytoYou.com

Email:

margh@yourjourneytoyou.com

Facebook:

www.facebook.com/yourjourneytoyou

I Was Desperate to Have Someone in My Life

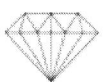

Margi Batson

Today I'm a FasterEFT practitioner, and I refer to myself as a 'Stress Relief Consultant.' Before that came about, however, life was very different. My experiences are unique to me, but I am willing to share my story if I can help someone else to handle their challenges and to overcome.

I'd have breathed for if I was asked.

I was many-years married, safe, secure, and retired from full-time work. I was enjoying my leisure time and about to become a nanna for the first time. Life was good. Then suddenly, and without warning, it all changed. The man I had loved unconditionally, who I trusted, believed in, and who I'd have breathed for if I was asked, told me he was leaving our marriage. Within 2 weeks he had packed his bags and walked out of my life.

After my husband, left, I was in a state of shock, confused, depressed, and grieving. I didn't know how to move on or how to pull myself out of the very dark place I was in. He and I had met when we were 18, started 'courting' at 19, and then married in 1970 when we were both 23. We had our first daughter 3 years later and then our second daughter 3 years after that. I thought our marriage was water tight. Several friends had separated, but I firmly believed that would never happen to us.

We'd certainly had challenges throughout our marriage - not so much with our relationship, but with work and business experiences. We'd stuck together through it all and supported each other. I could never imagine that we would ever be apart. How wrong I was. After 43 years, my husband told me he wanted to 'live on his own,' and, after a few upsetting discussions, he packed his bags and moved out. Shortly thereafter I found out he had moved in with a woman 25 years his junior. How did I handle this? Not very well. The bottom had literally dropped out of my world.

For so many years, my husband and I did most things as a couple. Each weekend we would either have someone over for a BBQ or we would be invited to their place. We had a holiday shack that we shared with others, and we often stayed for the weekend. We had some different interests, of course. He had his car racing and I enjoyed art, but for the most part we did everything together. But after he left, nothing was the same anymore, and everything that had been familiar to me had vanished. The old routines - such as meeting my husband for coffee or lunch, and speaking on the phone while he was at work – were gone. Our evening routine, where he would cook dinner and I would sit at our kitchen bench and ask him about his day, was no longer.

I was in a deep, dark depression, struggling to understand or come to terms with what he had done.

Now completely on my own, I was in a deep, dark depression, struggling to understand or come to terms with what he had done. I felt abandoned, betrayed, lied to, and deceived by the one person I would have given my life for. How could this be happening? I went through every extreme emotion possible: anger, hurt, confusion, betrayal. I was a mess. My moods were also impacting both of my daughters who were upset, confused, and wondering what had happened to parents who they thought would be together forever. I would get into my car and just drive for hours, with no direction and no purpose.

I didn't exist and no one was interested in me.

I was a danger to myself and others, as I was in shock and traumatised. If I wasn't driving, I was home crying endlessly day and night. I felt so isolated and alone - and to add insult to injury, my mother-in-law, who had been a part of my life for all those years, didn't contact me to see if I was OK. It was as if I didn't exist and no one was interested in me.

Two years after my husband left, the initial shock had dispersed, but feeling lonely and, in desperation, I joined several internet dating sites, wondering if this was the way to go. Would meeting other people help get me out of the depressed state? In actuality, I met a lot of very lonely people, but eventually I connected with one man in particular. We started seeing each other on a regular basis. I enjoyed his company - we laughed, we played, we travelled together, and it was good to have someone to connect with on a social level. I was smitten, and then I found out that he was a serial dater. He had no less than 4 other ladies in his life.

> I was desperate to have someone in my life
> and not be on my own.

Once again I was hurt and demoralized, but I continued seeing him as our time together was fun, and, besides, I was desperate to have someone in my life and not be on my own. But the relationship was a roller coaster ride and was doomed from the start. We went on an extended holiday, and when we returned I never heard from him again. No comments, no explanation, and, once again, I was abandoned and betrayed.

My emotional state was affecting my daughters - and I knew I had to pull myself out of it, not just for my own well-being but for them as well. I had past experience with various emotional healing modalities and decided to immerse myself in study again. One day, I came across FasterEFT on some YouTube videos and did the 7-day free trial. I was impressed with the results, and without hesitation I bought the home study course. In less than 6 months, I'd achieved the Level 3 certification, both with home study and by attending training seminars in person.

I committed to continued study and achieving higher levels. I set up a practice working out of a lovely room at my daughter's Pilates studio. Over the past 2 years I've had many clients with a variety of problems both physical and emotional, and I'm humbled to say that after several sessions they have all had good and lasting results. My business continues to grow through word of mouth.

Where to from here? Six years after my marriage breakup, I've recently had to sell and move out of my beautiful apartment. I'd been hanging onto it by the skin of my teeth, but finances were such that it was no longer viable to stay there. If I want to continue to live in the comfortable situation that I've become accustomed to, I need to continue to work - another challenging thought as I'll be 70 next birthday. I do have my FasterEFT skills and knowledge, and that is something that I will be focusing on in the future.

In the interim, I visit my UK daughter each year, and that costs money. I've decided to take on extra work and have registered with a caring agency in the UK. After exhaustive training, I'm now a certified carer. I'm currently caring for an elderly lady who's been diagnosed with Parkinson's disease and scoliosis - and also breathing problems which turn into anxiety and panic attacks. Her doctors were unable to help with the breathing, and when I mentioned I was a stress relief consultant, she asked if I could help her. With our sessions, she's learning to manage her breathing and to relax, and she's gaining confidence and control. If my personal circumstances were different, would I choose to take on the extra caring work? Probably not. I'm apprehensive about it all, but I'm up for the challenge. I find it a privilege to serve others - to help support and encourage people through a difficult stage of life and help them to keep dignity and grace intact. That is my aim.

The caring work is only for a few months, after which I'll head back home again and resume my FasterEFT consulting work. The Habilitat rehabilitation centre in Hawaii, where FasterEFT practitioners volunteer twice a year, is a pit stop for me on my way home. I've been selected as one of the practitioners to participate in the boot camp in January 2017, and that will be the icing on the cake.

These days, when I reflect on my long marriage, I see it all so differently. I knew it wasn't perfect, but I had accepted the imperfections. Now with my FasterEFT skills and knowledge, I can see the continuing patterns throughout that led to the breakup. They had been there right from the start. I also know that if I start to get upset about it all, it's just a story, it's not real, and I can laugh at myself. I've come a long way. I've had experiences that I wouldn't have chosen to have, but I'm so grateful that I did as they've helped me to become a stronger, wiser, and much more grounded individual. Although upsetting at the time, all these life experiences help give me more understanding and empathy with others.

It made me re-assess my life. I now see his actions as a gift

---

By using the FasterEFT techniques created by Robert G. Smith, I was able to heal and overcome my grief and depression. I was angry, bitter, and hurt by my husband's decision to leave. He didn't maintain contact and I struggled to understand how he could just walk away. Today I am so grateful for his decision. It made me re-assess my life and question who I am, where I was going, and what I wanted to do and to be. I now see his actions as a gift and an opportunity for me to grow and to learn. I have a very different outlook and mindset, and it's so liberating.

Margi Batson lives in Australia and is a qualified counsellor and a Level 3 FasterEFT practitioner. She has also studied Transcendental Meditation, dowsing, reflexology, and numerous other modalities. She is a qualified massage instructor, including the specialty of infant massage.

When her marriage of 40-plus years disintegrated, Margi was depressed and grieving, and didn't know how to move on or pull herself out of a very dark and depressed state. She found FasterEFT, and by using the techniques she watched on Robert G Smith's YouTube channel 'HealingMagic,' was able to heal and overcome grief and depression in a very short space of time. She now sees that traumatic experience as an opportunity to understand others in a similar situation.

Margi continues to study and to learn, and is always keen to add to her knowledge and skills. Her work as a FasterEFT practitioner is conducted from a lovely room at Encore Pilates in Darwin. She offers a free 30-minute consultation. If you are ready to schedule a session, contact her to make an appointment. She guarantees support, guidance, encouragement, accountability - and teaching a set of tools that have potential to change your life if applied consistently.

Website:
www.findyourpower.com.au

Email:
mjbats@gmail.com

Telephone:
(+61) 401 993 576

You Are Never Too Old to Learn

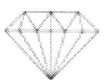

Marilyn J Porter

Who am I? What is my purpose to this life?

At the end of 2012 something happened that made me look at my life and start asking questions. The main question was 'Who am I?' and the second was 'What is my purpose to this life?'

Nobody had really showed me how to do it.

Over the years there are many things that I did to try to change my perception of who I thought I was. I had gone from being 'very religious' to 'spiritual.' I had tried most things out there, and, had the money been available, I would have gone to India to an ashram for true spiritual learning. I had attended every workshop that anyone would put on. I had learnt that a lot of my beliefs were 'in my head' and that I had the ability to change whatever I wanted to in my life - but nobody had really showed me how to do it.

In 2013 I was learning about my body and healthy eating. During a visit to Queensland, where all my children and grandchildren live, I heard of a seminar with three amazing entrepreneurial women. Attending this seminar triggered a lot of lost information that I had learnt many years ago on my quests. I started searching again for an answer.

A powerful, charismatic, dynamic speaker.

My search also took me to Greece where I attended a manifesting course with another amazing woman, Dr Michelle Neilson. In this course I wrote that I was 'a powerful, charismatic, dynamic speaker.' This was quite a statement at the time, as I had absolutely no idea on how I was going to go about becoming a powerful, charismatic, dynamic speaker.

Growing up I was known to have the 'gift of the gab.' I loved meeting and mixing with positive people. In 1982, I joined a well-known multi-level marketing corporation and became a bit of a success working that business. Due to my personality, I had a lot of friends within the business. One of the major things I learnt was that I could get up in front of people and empower them to work to their best potential.

Unfortunately, I never had a great belief in myself. I had very low self-esteem. When I was at school I was fearful of exams. I also couldn't understand why I needed to learn this unnecessary stuff. I was a dreamer, so my mind was always out of the window.

In 5th Class primary, when I was around 10 to 11 years old, we were given the assignment to write and talk about our dads' work. Until then I never knew that I had the gift of standing in front of crowds and presenting. Dad worked in the power stations, and when he heard about my assignment, he took me there. He explained how it worked, and then we drew diagrams and worked on a speech. This was my very first presentation, and it went so well that the teacher gave me the lead for the end-of-year play called 'Little Red Riding Hood.' The seed was planted.

I dropped out due to my fear of exams.

I do not remember much about my years at school, but I dropped out before the end of my final year due to my fear of exams and my belief that I was dumb and stupid. I have never attended any other school system. The fear in me was too great.

At the end of 2013, I was still searching for something. I always loved going to seminars and learning from the remarkable speakers at these events. I have owned a computer since the middle of the 1990's. I was fascinated with YouTube, so it was natural for me to gravitate and search for exceptional speakers on YouTube and follow what they had to teach.

I was working through money blocks with various practitioners on YouTube when I came across FasterEFT. I went into 'Healing Magic,' the YouTube site of Robert G. Smith.

Wow, it seemed that I had finally hit the jackpot. Everything I had learnt over the years from hypnosis, meridians, and many more modalities were amazingly brought together. I watched Robert's videos for over a month. Then he had a special on for the Home Study Kit which included 5 hours with an advanced practitioner, Deidre Maguire. I weighed it up and waited until the last possible moment before I purchased the kit. I had figured that I couldn't lose, and I would finally get to work on some of my core beliefs.

I bought the kit at the end of 2013, and it was a life changing event for me. In the 3 years that I have been a FasterEFT practitioner, I have gone from being unsure of myself to being just what I envisioned in the manifesting course in Greece - a very powerful, charismatic, dynamic speaker!

In 2015 I was invited by Robert to be part of an amazing group to go to a substance abuse centre in Hawaii called Habilitat. This was a great honour for me, as I wanted so much to learn the FasterEFT protocol for drug and alcohol addictions.

Robert invites and takes 10 of his best practitioners from all over the world to Habilitat twice a year to work with the residents and help them overcome their addictions. Using the Faster EFT modality, these residents have the chance to change the emotional triggers which have kept them in their substance for many years. The success of Habilitat is very high. I know that 5 years ago they had a 65 percent success rate.

The questions that I have asked myself over the years are now being answered. So how has FasterEFT changed my life?

can you Believe it !

> I have gone from a woman who had no direction in her life,
> to one who has direction.

I have gone from a very tearful, unsure person to a very confident one. I have gone from a woman who had no direction in her life, to one who has direction.

I have gone from a woman who was looking, and not sure which way to turn, to one who is empowered and has purpose. I have gone from that lost little girl, who used to dream of becoming someone famous, to being famous in my own right.

And now that I have the drive and desire not to give up, I am going to live to over 100 years young and will continue to follow my dream!

> Life happens quickly and is too short to mull over the small stuff.

We are only here for such a short time. I think of my mum, who is nearly 92 years young. It must seem to her like only yesterday that she was that young girl playing and having fun with her siblings, then a blushing bride, and then a young mum of three daughters. In time she was a married woman of 65 years and then a widow at the age of 86. She became a grandmother, great-grandmother, and a great-great grandmother. Life happens quickly and is too short to mull over the small stuff. It is time for all of you to find the passion that is within you and to change your world for a better and brighter tomorrow.

Three years ago, I met over Skype a beautiful woman named Deirdre Maguire who lives in Newcastle, County Down, in Ireland. I live in Newcastle, NSW, Australia. The similarities are amazing. Who would have thought that in three short years I would become an Advanced Level 4 FasterEFT practitioner who has a lot of confidence and knowledge? Who would have thought that my life would be changed forever by the many wonderful practitioners who have worked with me to help create those many changes?

In my late 60's, life is changing all the time for the better.

I failed in English. I couldn't spell if my life depended on it, and here I am putting pen to paper. Now, at the wonderful age of my late 60's, life is changing all the time for the better. And I love that I am now able to help 'change one person at a time' from anywhere around the world. The amount of people that are being helped with this modality is amazing.

What is it you want from your life? Do you believe that life is passing you by and that it is too late to change? You too can change your life. Go out and find that spark that you were born with. Have a dream and make a success of it.

At the end of 2012, Marilyn found herself in a bad place. She knew that she needed to make changes within herself, so she went on a self-discovery journey. At the end of 2013, she found Faster Emotionally Focused Transformations (FasterEFT) created by Robert G Smith.

Seeking to constantly improve herself and help her clients, Marilyn became an Advanced, Level 4 FasterEFT practitioner, a clinical hypnotherapist, and an author.

As part of the requirements to becoming an advanced FasterEFT practitioner, Marilyn found that she had to continually work on clearing her own programs. This has helped her become very successful within her field. Marilyn is now working with clients all over the world. She is also presenting the FasterEFT modality to groups through free talks and seminars.

Marilyn's passion is to help as many people around the world as possible, who are ready to discover their own true potential by realising and changing the long-held beliefs they have about themselves. She likes to quote Robert Smith in saying that she is helping to change 'one person at a time.'

Marilyn offers a complimentary 30-minute consultation. She works either face- to-face or over Skype or Zoom.

Website:

www.healingbyfastereft.com

Email:

marilyn@healingbyfastereft.com

I Wished I'd Never Heard of FasterEFT!

Myroulla Mallouppa

What brought me here? How did I end up being a FasterEFT practitioner travelling the world giving sessions, doing volunteer work, and giving seminars on my own? Though sometimes it's hard for me to believe, this is my reality today.

I thought I would get more love if I was ill.

I grew up in a family where being sick equalled love and attention. My father had problems with his stomach, and my mother had to cook special food for him. My brother had the same problems, so my mother had to cook special food for him too. Somehow I thought I would get more love or special attention if I was also ill. I started going through surgeries at the age of 2, and with some of the operations it was 'border-line' whether I was going to make it or not.

By the age of 40, I had been operated on approximately 14 times.

By the age of 40, I had been operated on approximately 14 times. In my early twenties, I had a major operation for my intestines because they felt 'stuck' and paralyzed, and the doctors had to operate on me urgently.

After the surgery they stated they didn't really know what was going on, but they did say, 'It's stress, you can't do anything about it, and if it happens again, you will have to have surgery again.' When it did start to happen again, that's when I decided, 'I can't do it! I can't sit and wait for it to happen all over!' I need to do something, now!

I knew I needed help, so I started counseling and talk therapy, and I was attending all kinds of seminars and workshops. I was feeling better and making some progress, but often the same pattern of feelings and beliefs were showing up, and I was still undergoing surgeries. I was getting to a point where I was feeling 'this is just not working for me.' I was also a heavy smoker and had asthma, so my doctor suggested that I go to a woman who did hands-on healing to help me quit smoking. I did go, and I did quit smoking! Then she did other energy healing for me, which also helped me.

This was a big turning point, so I started getting to know alternative therapies. Two years later I came across an energy healing technique that I decided to get trained in myself. I became a practitioner, which was another big turning point. Soon I started teaching, having clients, and seeing more changes in my life - but still something was missing.

can you Believe it !

One day, a friend told me about a method he believed would add to my practice. It was called FasterEFT. He had sent me some links for the YouTube videos, but to be honest I never looked at them. Then when my friend called to say he was going to a 'Transformational Weekend' seminar for FasterEFT, I had to tell him I couldn't go, because I had just had an operation on my knee. But something was changing inside me, because it turned out this would be my last surgery, even though I didn't know it at the time.

When my friend called another time, saying that there was going to be a FasterEFT Level 1 training in Europe, in Budapest, it took me 10 minutes to decide that I was going. And within another 10 minutes I had booked everything - flights, hotel, and seminar.

---

*What I learned at the FasterEFT seminar made so much sense!
And it was like learning a new language.*

Going to my FasterEFT Level 1 training, I didn't have many expectations as I didn't really know what it was all about. I thought it was just another empowering seminar. I trusted my friend who said it would add to my knowledge and practice, but I never expected it would turn out to be a life-changing experience. What I learned at the FasterEFT seminar made so much sense! I learned new things and got to understand more about how the mind works. It was very interesting, and it was like learning a new language. But at the same time it was scary, because I knew that I was going to change if I used FasterEFT. The principles of this method say that everything is in YOU! In fact, it's JUST you - every character, every word, and every feeling.

> I had CHOSEN to be a victim.

Nobody had made me a victim. I had CHOSEN to be a victim. Oh my Goodness! I thought I was in a good space, but it turned out I wasn't as much as I thought I was! FasterEFT taught me that I needed to change many things and I needed to take responsibility.

> There were times when I wished I'd never heard of FasterEFT.

There were times when I wished I'd never heard of FasterEFT. It was so much easier to blame others and keep my comfortable role of victim. Going back home after the FasterEFT Level 1 seminar, I thought, 'Okay, I trained in FasterEFT, but I don't necessarily need to use it. I can put it aside and continue my practice as I used to do.' But it didn't work out this way.

Whether I wanted it or not, it was becoming part of my life and my practice. And I think the reason is that with FasterEFT, things started to make sense. I had started to realize my patterns of behavior, my beliefs, and how my beliefs were actually determining my life.

My 'wants' can become my 'haves.'

Having to write down my 'peace list,' in order to see what I needed to make peace with and release, was quite a shock for me. Writing my life down, I could see all the pain I was holding. I could also see the same patterns showing up everywhere - the same patterns 'in a different pair of shoes' as I learned at the seminar. But in dealing with each of my past difficult memories, I started experiencing changes in my life, getting more into it, studying more about it, going to every seminar, having sessions on myself, giving sessions to others, feeling better, and looking better. I wanted to get rid of as many old beliefs as I could. And I had come to a new realization: My 'wants' can become my 'haves.'

I set up an intention just two years ago in Budapest at the FasterEFT Seminar, Level 1. Watching Deirdre Maguire sharing her story about how her life has changed with FasterEFT stirred something inside me. Deirdre was travelling the world, teaching people, and giving FasterEFT sessions - and I told myself, 'In two years I will be doing the same.'

Somehow I had totally forgotten this promise to myself, but almost exactly two years later, I received an invitation to give a seminar on 'success' to 40 women management assistants. Without much deliberating I accepted the invitation, believing that I would partner with a business associate for the seminar. He couldn't join me, however, so I did the seminar on my own. 'You can do it,' I kept telling myself. I needed not only many hours of preparation, but lots of FasterEFT sessions to help me remove my fears and my negative beliefs, two of which were 'I can't do it on my own' and 'I don't know how.'

But I DID do it on my own. And while giving my first solo seminar I realized my promise to myself from two years earlier. I realized it was happening!

What have I accomplished? Since the 'success' workshop earlier this year, I can't believe how much I've done. Just one month later, I organized and hosted a seminar for Robert in Cyprus. Then I traveled to Athens to do another seminar. In June, I travelled to India, twice, to do FasterEFT sessions.

In July, I travelled to Hawaii to volunteer at Habilitat, giving sessions to people recovering from drug addiction. Right after Habilitat, I trained in Dublin, Ireland, to become a corporate health and wellness consultant. After that, I made a third trip to India to continue sessions with my clients. All of this intensive participation in FasterEFT activities has paid off, because I was recently able to achieve my latest goal of becoming a Level 4 FasterEFT Advanced Practitioner!

Today, I'm living my dream. It's happening! I am travelling the world, giving sessions, teaching, and doing volunteer work! And now I often say that I will do whatever it takes to be out there to experience my wants, my goals and to live my dream. And this is only the beginning!

Myroulla Mallouppa is a True Success Strategist and a corporate trainer. She continues to enrich her expertise by attending specialized seminars, trainings, and workshops around the world – and also travels extensively to assist clients.

Her goal is to facilitate transformation at the deepest level and help people to eliminate stress, improve the quality of their lives, and achieve their personal and professional goals. Through her compassionate and comprehensive approach, she helps individuals and corporate clients to move forward in their personal lives and careers.

Myroulla believes the key to transforming lives is to discover the root of the non-beneficial patterns, facilitate transformation, and then help people to take control of their physical, emotional, and financial health.

Her clients claim that her personality, expertise, knowledge, and passion compose a powerful formula that makes miracles happen. She works with people experiencing a variety of issues - physical, emotional, and sexual abuse; drug, food, and alcohol addictions; eating disorders; broken relationships; depression, anxiety, fears, and phobias; and more. She adores her work and pledges to keep doing her best to help her clients free their minds and open the door to endless possibilities for their futures!

Website:

www.myroullamallouppa.com

Email:

myroulla@myroullamallouppa.com

Telephone:

+357 99 646 746

Facebook Page:

www.facebook.com/MyroullaMallouppa.TrueSuccessStrategist

Skype Name:

Myroul

LinkedIn:

https://www.linkedin.com/in/myroulla-mallouppa-59787b18

Instagram: https://www.instagram.com/myroullamallouppa

Twitter:

https://twitter.com/MYROUL

can you Believe it !

FasterEFT and Financial Transformation

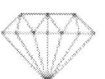

Odille Rault

I always ended up struggling.

I'd had a pattern of financial struggle for as long as I could remember. It seemed that no matter how hard I worked, or how much I changed my actions, decisions, and beliefs about money, I always ended up struggling – against all odds. When I did earn more money, my car would break down, I would get ill, a job would be cancelled, or someone wouldn't pay me – whatever negative event it took to bring me back in alignment with financial struggle.

It was something INSIDE me.

Over the years, I went from believing I needed to somehow physically change my situation – work harder, save more, reduce my outgoings, or do different work – to realising that it was something INSIDE me. I had learned that even when I did exactly what people who succeeded did, I would fail. It really had nothing to do with the outside world; it was about my own beliefs.

> I took all the practical action I could. And still, I struggled.

I continued, for years, to strive to change what I was doing – both practically and on a spiritual level. However, even when things would appear to improve for a period of time, something (that appeared to be completely beyond my control) would occur to take me back into the status quo of struggle. I changed my beliefs around money – I genuinely believed in abundance. I studied the Law of Attraction. I tried countless modalities and therapies. I took all the practical action I could. And still, I struggled.

> BUT . . . I was still struggling financially.

Many rock-bottom moments and much frustration eventually led to my discoveries about self-love and the power of unconditional love. From these discoveries, and based on my success in other areas of my life, I developed my own modality. This changed my life dramatically! I went from a life of drama, turmoil, stress and fibromyalgia to happier and healthier than I'd ever been before! BUT . . . I was still struggling financially. Although my financial situation was not quite as dramatic as it had been in the past, I was still unable to pay my bills; I was still struggling with people not paying me on time (and sometimes not at all).

Finally, in September 2015, having studied and tried so many other options (most recently, neuroscience) I watched a video my sister had forwarded to me. It was a YouTube video of Robert G. Smith explaining how the mind works. As I watched it, everything he was saying made perfect sense. It explained exactly why I had experienced the financial struggles I had – despite all my efforts.

As Robert went through the explanation of the effects of memories (subconscious records) on our lives, the information he was sharing fitted in perfectly with what I already knew about the brain and body.

I noticed how it felt,

and then recognised the feeling from early experiences.

I continued to watch the YouTube videos of FasterEFT, getting progressively more excited and gaining a fuller understanding of how it worked. I started tapping along, and could feel a definite shift. I decided to address the money issues specifically.

Following Robert's guidance from his YouTube videos, I asked myself: How do I know I have a money problem? The answer was: Because I never seem to have enough to pay my bills. My next question to myself was: And how does that feel? I noticed how it felt, and then recognised the feeling from early experiences.

It had nothing to do with money, but it was the same feeling. I didn't have any specific memories; it was just an overall feeling. So I simply noticed it, and then I used the FasterEFT technique to tap on it.

> This is never going to end!

I cried (a lot!) and it seemed to go on forever. In the middle of it, I thought to myself: 'This is never going to end! I'm going to be like this for the rest of my life!' I knew logically that it was not possible for me to stay like that for the rest of my life; but it certainly felt as though there was no way it would ever end. I kept tapping through the sobs. At one point, during that first tapping session, I wanted to give up and just go to bed and continue crying. But I knew, intellectually, that I needed to keep going. So I did.

> After about 45 minutes, the feeling flipped.
> It all flipped to peace and unconditional love.

After about 45 minutes, the feeling flipped. I went from the intense negative emotions to feeling peace and unconditional love. I was drained, but I knew I'd experienced a massive shift. The next day, something occurred to me I hadn't realised before. It was a belief that I hadn't been aware of before then, and I sat down and addressed it using FasterEFT. Again, it was a longer session than I expected. Again, it was a massive emotional response, but this time, laughing! I laughed, out loud, for around 40 minutes as I tapped. I knew at the time that the laughing was the body's emotional release. Towards the end of 40 minutes, the intense emotions and laughter subsided; and again, it all flipped to peace and unconditional love.

I wanted to see a FasterEFT practitioner. I knew I couldn't afford it, but I was determined to find a way. I found that Carol Langdon, a Level 3 FasterEFT practitioner, lived the closest to me, and I contacted her to find out how much she charged. I didn't have the money, but I was determined to prioritise what I knew was the key to changing my financial patterns.

I continued to tap on myself; and as I worked through the various issues and memories, I started to notice little changes. Soon, I ended up earning £126 more than I was expecting for a particular job. I immediately booked my first session with Carol, and made the 90-minute drive from my home to see her.

The session was different to what I'd expected. Having only seen the videos of Robert on YouTube, I hadn't been aware of the full intake and process of a private session. It was amazing, and Carol was warm, supportive, and an expert guide throughout. Again, I noticed little changes after doing this work – a few more small unexpected amounts of money, and a change in my confidence and sense of self-worth.

I decided to adopt a 'zero tolerance' attitude.

From then on, I decided to adopt a 'zero tolerance' attitude. I made the commitment to myself to tap on absolutely everything that bothered me. No matter what the topic was, and no matter how small it seemed, I would tap - right then, in the moment. So, I started to do that! There were times when I almost let things slide. I would catch a fleeting thought that I barely noticed, and find myself starting to ignore it. However, I would then choose to tap it out in the moment.

I believe that, although the session I'd had with Carol, and the two big sessions I'd done on my own, had resulted in massive shifts, it was this 'zero tolerance' attitude that was crucial in creating the greatest change for me.

I woke up thinking differently.

I had been wanting to attend a live FasterEFT training ever since I had first watched the videos. There was one coming up in Malaga, Spain, in February 2016; but I had no idea where the money would come from.

One morning, a few days after starting the 'zero tolerance,' I woke up thinking differently. I started thinking in ways I hadn't thought before, and I noticed opportunities I hadn't noticed before. The result was an almost overnight increase in my income by around 500 percent!

I continued to tap out all of the doubts and fears that came with this new financial experience. I was very aware that there was still a lot that needed to be addressed. I knew that previous experiences of an increase in income had resulted in 'something' happening to recreate the status quo of struggle - so I continued the 'zero tolerance' policy, and tapped on every doubt and fearful thought that came up.

I began to tap out the stress 'fight-or-flight' state that occurred just before sending an invoice. I made sure that I didn't send the invoice until I had flipped that anxiety to peace and unconditional love. I noticed the thoughts: 'It won't last'; 'It'll all go wrong' and 'I won't get paid.' And I tapped on each one until it flipped.

In February, 2016 – just five months after I watched that first YouTube video – I attended the Level 1 FasterEFT training in Oklahoma City, USA. A few months before, I had no idea how I would pay my bills. Now, I was flying to America to attend a live seminar!

It was everything I'd imagined, and more.

It was everything I'd imagined, and more. In addition to gaining a deeper understanding of FasterEFT from the training, I also had two 'cross-fire' sessions with practitioners Heather McKean and Tiffany Jeffers. (A cross-fire is a session with two or more practitioners - and it is more intense and deeper work than a 'regular' session.) These two sessions transformed key programs in me that connected my self-worth and money. The results were mind-blowing, and my life continued to improve.

Now, in just under 12 months since I watched that first video, I have gone from being unable to pay my bills, to travelling to the USA (twice), Spain, Greece, and Ireland! And I'll be attending the Level 3 FasterEFT Training in Oklahoma City just a few weeks from now. I am earning a great income doing what I love, I'm happier and healthier than I've ever been before, and I am moving forward with my passions – without the stress, doubts, and struggle that would have accompanied me in the past.

I am loving using FasterEFT in combination with my own modality (using unconditional love as a power) to help others free and empower themselves so they may live the lives they truly desire and deserve.

Odille is an Empowerment Coach, Author, and Inspirational Speaker, specialising in the power of unconditional love. Her books (THE MAGIC PILL; THE SECOND DOSE; BEYOND THE MAGIC PILL and YOU HAVE A SUPERPOWER) and workshops have empowered countless people to develop the skills of using unconditional love - for the self and others - as a power, to transform all areas of life.

Odille recently founded the CHURCH OF UNCONDITIONAL LOVE, taking her mission of sharing the power of unconditional love and FasterEFT to the next level.

Websites:

www.emotionalstatemastery.com

www.yourselfempowered.com

www.churchofunconditionallove.com

Facebook:

www.facebook.com/churchofunconditionallove

www.facebook.com/beyondthemagicpill

can you Believe it !

My Daughter's Cancer, FasterEFT, and a $120,000+ Hospital Bill

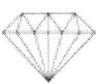

Olga Bochareva

I have always believed in miracles.

I am a certified FasterEFT practitioner. My work is not only my profession, but also my passion. When people ask me what I do, I readily talk to them about FasterEFT. But when I'm asked what I do for a living, I often simply answer that **'I watch miracles happen.'**

September 18th, 2015 - the day my 2 ½-year-old daughter, Vicky was abruptly diagnosed with leukemia. I felt like time stopped for a moment.

Yes, that's what I often DID say, until . . . September 18th, 2015 - the day my 2 ½-year-old daughter, Vicky was abruptly diagnosed with leukemia. She was a perfectly healthy child who barely ever had a cold. I remember first hearing the news from our pediatrician while I was in the DSW store shopping for shoes with my mom. When I heard the doctor speak those words about my daughter, I felt like time stopped for a moment. I just thought, 'This is a mistake.' Unfortunately, it wasn't. The doctor asked us to her office straightaway to discuss the situation and to let us know that we needed to check Vicky into the hospital THAT DAY! So, we went home, packed our bags, and drove to the MD Anderson Cancer Hospital, here in Houston, that same evening.

On top of that devastating news, we came to discover that our insurance was extremely bad, as it turned out, and did not cover even 20 percent of the hospital bill. So at that moment we were facing $120,000-plus in medical bills for just the initial 2 weeks of Vicky's hospital stay.

My world had come crashing down. Everything I used to believe about FasterEFT and the law of attraction was now failing me.

None of what was happening at that time made sense. All I wanted to do every single day was to 'hit the reset button' and wake up from the nightmare. Instead, every morning I'd wake up and have to face – all over again - the dark reality of Vicky being pumped with chemo, while we had no clue how we were going to pay for it all.

So being the proactive person I am, I applied for a government grant to cover the expenses to fund the treatment - and I started tapping. I scheduled a 2-hour FasterEFT session with my practitioner, and after LOTS of tears and tapping, I got clarity on what I wanted at that moment:

There were two things I was tapping on:

1. Seeing my daughter perfectly healthy with a full head of hair, and walking to the bus stop to catch the school bus.

2. Looking at our hospital bills and seeing '0' (zero dollars) on

can you Believe it !

all the balances.

Needless to say, at that time it was nearly impossible for me to tap into any of these future visions. In the 2-month initial period of Vicky's treatment, there was lots of uncertainty. She was in and out of hospital, and we were not sure what to believe about her health prognosis. In the middle of this terribly stressful situation, we received the $120,000 bill from the hospital. I still remember staring at the letter in disbelief. My husband was not coping well with the situation overall, so I had to take over all bills and paper work and figure out what to do.

In order to go on, I had to literally ignore my reality. I was clear about what I didn't want. I didn't want Vicky to have cancer! But in the middle of this overwhelming situation, it was hard to figure out what I DID want. This is why I hired a FasterEFT practitioner to help me tap and to help me focus on that.

Things started to turn around.

Things started to turn around. On November 3rd, I received a phone call from our financial adviser from the hospital. Our grant to fund Vicky's treatment was approved. **One hundred percent of Vicky's hospital bills will be paid in full for the entire year. (Yep, over $120,000!)**

Today, less than a year later, my daughter is in remission and perfectly happy and healthy.

Today, less than a year later, my daughter is in remission and perfectly happy and healthy. She still continues the treatment (as part of the medical protocol) and her hair has not grown back just yet. But she is doing amazing, is full of energy, is pain free - and is just a tiny walking blessing!

If this is not a miracle, I don't know what is.

Learning how to master your mind
is the best skill you can possibly acquire.

Faster EFT works, because your mind is the most powerful tool you have for creating change. And learning how to master your mind - so you can manifest what you want and need - is the best skill you can possibly acquire.

This experience taught me that 99 percent of the manifesting process is not complete until I see any physical evidence.

So whatever you are facing in your life, know that you CAN change that if you persevere.
Keep on tapping my friend! I will be!
It really does work.

Olga Bochareva is a corporate health and wellness consultant, as well as a Level 3 FasterEFT practitioner. She lives in Texas, in the United States, and works with people, both in person and via Skype, to help them achieve their dreams - whether in their personal lives or in their businesses.

Olga is deeply passionate about fearless living and believes that danger is real, but fear is a choice. Her clients are heart-centered coaches, yoga studio owners, biz coaches, published authors, and TED Talk speakers. She is an enthusiastic coach who works with entrepreneurs and entrepreneurs-in-training to help them release emotional hang-ups, fears, and doubts so they can create the 'biz' and life they are hungry for. Her 'CEO Mindset' approach helps her focus her clients toward success.

Website:

www.OlgaBochareva.com

I Didn't Know if My Dreams Were Really Possible

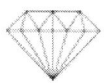

Pat Studstill

I would love to share my story of how I used FasterEFT to completely change my life. I have shared testimonials before about how my health improved dramatically going from bedridden (and diagnosed with multiple medical issues) to a return to much better health and living again. But, there is so much more to my story.

Just prior to becoming bedridden and toxic with arsenic, I had asked for a divorce. I had been married for 18 years at that time and had endured treacherous treatment, including my husband's affair. It took another 5 years and overcoming many obstacles to extract myself from that marriage.

By the time the divorce was final, I was left bankrupt, no job nor job history, and still very sick. And I learned that everything we had built together had been completely dismantled. Obstacles were being put in my way to keep me trapped in the marriage, including financial abuse - such as running up credit card bills, in my name, which I had no way to pay.

> I used FasterEFT on every doubt, every fear, and every strategy that was designed to keep me trapped within that marriage.

It was during those 5 years of struggle to leave the marriage that I began using FasterEFT on a regular basis. Because of FasterEFT, I was able to regain emotional stability, even to the point of having the confidence to file my own bankruptcy without legal counsel, since I couldn't even afford to hire a bankruptcy lawyer. I used FasterEFT on every doubt, every fear, and every strategy that was designed to keep me trapped within that marriage.

My daughter was systematically turned against me and rejected me completely, cutting me off from my grandson. Even through that potentially devastating experience, I used FasterEFT to restore my peace. I was able to release the hurt and send loving messages on a regular basis to her without expectations. Recently, I was invited (and attended) my grandson's birthday party. That might never have happened if it weren't for FasterEFT.

During the 5-year ordeal of trying to leave the marriage, I created a dream/goal vision board of what I wanted my future to look like and become. At the very top I placed a picture that represented peace with the words 'I live in PEACE' written over it. I added a picture of 2 hands connecting across the globe, because I wanted to find a way to touch people's lives around the world.

I added many more pictures to my board as a way to declare my intentions.

can you Believe it !

I placed the board where I could see it. I used FasterEFT when I meditated on that vision board. I used FasterEFT to heal all the emotional pain from the failed marriage and to heal my childhood wounds that kept me from understanding and being able to accept real love. I used FasterEFT to heal my physical symptoms and chronic illnesses.

I am in complete peace within my marriage.

Today, I am living my dreams! I am now married to a man who loves me very deeply and unconditionally. It is incredibly amazing to be able to trust your partner completely, knowing that they are guarding your heart as much as you are guarding theirs. I am in complete peace within my marriage. I also live in a beautifully peaceful setting on a lake. Every day, I get to share the wonderful gift of FasterEFT with others around the world.

I didn't know if my dreams were really possible.

Most of the items on my vision board have become a reality in my life. I am now adding new things. Looking back, it is amazing at how far I have come! At the time I created my vision board, I didn't know if my dreams were really possible, but with FasterEFT, we let go of everything that is holding us back from living our best life. Then nothing is in the way of living the life of our dreams! By letting go, we truly become free to live.

Pat lives in the state of Georgia, located in the south-eastern region of the United States, and is a certified Level 4 FasterEFT practitioner working towards her Master Level certification.

Pat considers herself to be a life transformation expert, utilizing cutting-edge mind-body healing techniques to transform the lives of people struggling with chronic illnesses and stress to thriving in health and peace.

At her lowest, Pat was bedridden and living with multiple chronic illnesses - Lyme disease, fibromyalgia, Hashimoto's thyroiditis, chronic fatigue syndrome, a parathyroid tumour, and polycystic ovarian syndrome, to name just a few.

When she found FasterEFT, she was able to move from desperation, to relief, to thriving. Within a short time, she experienced astonishing results; and knew she wanted to share this amazing gift with others.

Pat works with clients regardless of location, using both Skype and phone, making sessions convenient both locally and internationally. Contact her if you would like to know more or you would like to book a free consultation.

Website:
www.freetolive.me

Email:
pat@freetolive.me

can you Believe it !

IT Was the Best Session I Ever Had

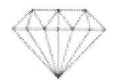

René Zorrilla

For more than a decade, I have been a practitioner of healing techniques for physical pain, emotions, and other issues. I don't consider this work, because it's my passion and what I love to do.

When I first began treating clients, I often used a form of acupuncture, then shiatsu massage, and then finished with a massage of the head. I continued to learn new techniques, so I had many good modalities that I could use. I had a good practice, and I was working a lot. But after 2 or 3 months, clients whose issues I thought were resolved came back for more treatment - and I noticed I had to work on the same complaint again. I started to realize that I wasn't working on the core of their problem.

Over time I realized that their problems were connected to their feelings.

I really wanted to solve this dilemma. I questioned my clients about their physical issues, and over time I realized that their problems were connected to their feelings. I realized that everything was feelings - sadness, anger, etc. So, I thought, I have to work on feelings in a more specific way. I decided to learn other techniques to do that, and I began to train myself on other techniques. All these techniques were good and effective in their way.

Then one day, I saw a one-hour video of Robert Smith using FasterEFT. The video was about why we become addicted. It was made in Habilitat, the addiction treatment centre in Hawaii, and it blew my mind. It changed my perspective.

So I bought the FasterEFT Ultimate Training Course on DVD. I did levels 1, 2, and 3 from this course, and then I invited Robert to come here, to Belgium, where he wanted to do a Transformational Weekend. It was great to meet Robert and talk with him in person, because I could see the potential and value of FasterEFT.

I went to Level 1 training several times, and then I did Level 2 and Level 3 in-person also. Eventually, I applied to volunteer at Habilitat, and this is where I accomplished my Level 4 certification.

I didn't have a large client base and I was always worried about paying my bills.

So how did FasterEFT help me, personally? Well it helped me tremendously to improve my business. I had a goal that one day I would be completely independent as a practitioner. At this time, I was working only part-time with clients, and I had no other job. Money was an issue. I felt insecure about my business and my finances in general because I didn't have enough clients at that point. I felt very stressed because I didn't have a large client base and I was always worried about paying my bills.

Then one day, I did a session without charge for someone who had no money to pay me. He was an astrologer, and he said, I will return the favor by preparing your astrological chart. I agreed, and I asked him, 'Can you help me to know the best time to launch my business?' He said, 'Yes, of course I can.' So he prepared my astrological chart, and then told me, 'You have the most favorable chart I've ever seen, but you have one problem. One of your planets indicates that you have a problem with money. And if you don't clean that up, you will do things that will blow the good parts of the chart.' And I said 'Oh S#!T.'

I think it was the best session I've ever had.

I knew I had a problem, but I felt it wasn't that serious, or that bad. But I decided to book a session with Deirdre Maguire, who I knew was the 'number two' person in FasterEFT because I had seen her on YouTube. At that time in my life, paying for this FasterEFT session was a big financial sacrifice for me. But I knew it was important, so I had a session with Deirdre on Skype. Since then, I've never regretted it. I think it was the best session I've ever had.

After a month, I had a 50 percent increase in my clients.

For that session with Deirdre, I wrote a 'peace list' so she would know what my issues were that needed to be addressed. Well, I was amazed by the way she made me 'travel through' the peace list. If I hadn't known what she was doing, I wouldn't have noticed. But because I knew the FasterEFT process, and I knew the 'art of change' that we use in FasterEFT, I knew what she was doing. It was like art. It was great, because it was smooth. And I have to say that after 2 hours, I really felt loved by Deirdre, and that was amazing. And another amazing thing is that 15 days after her session, I had an increase of 30 percent in my clients. After a month, I had a 50 percent increase in my clients. And since then, I have always had enough clients.

I made peace with that aspect of money.

That session changed a lot of things. It was a big, big, big shift for me at the time. It was like I made peace with that aspect of money. My beliefs changed, and in addition to the change regarding money, I had some other growth from that session. So it was worth every dollar or Euro I spent.

Then I was able to meet Deirdre in person. Now I consider her a friend, and I hope she feels the same. She's amazing. She's kind, she's sweet, she's lovely. And she really loves to help people. And she's a great person. In fact, I love her very much. I've told her a bunch of times, because for me it's important to let people I love know that I love them.

So now it's official! Deirdre, I love you! You're a great woman. So that's my story with her. When we talk or see each other, we have a lot of fun. We've had other sessions. I give her sessions, and she gives me sessions. We've spent a lot of time together. We have amazing hugs. We laugh a lot when we're together. Yeah, she's a great woman. I can't wait to see her work as a teacher. I haven't been able to go to any of her seminars, yet, but I plan to do it. And I would advise everyone to do it, because she's great. She's great as a practitioner, and she's a beautiful woman.

FasterEFT is faster and deeper.

So since I learned FasterEFT, I have turned to it almost completely when I work with clients. I use it 99.9 percent of the time. At first I would start a treatment with another modality and then finish with FasterEFT. Finally, after doing this for a while, I said 'Okay, it's over.' I turned completely to FasterEFT. I use FasterEFT 99.9 percent of the time now. It's very rare that I use others. The other methods are good, but FasterEFT is faster and deeper.

René Zorrilla lives in Belgium with his wife and son. For the last 10 years, he has studied and been a practitioner in various healing modalities, including acupuncture, osteopathy, and shiatsu massage.

René credits his first FasterEFT session with Deirdre Maguire with helping him to attract more clients and also with relieving blocks over money. He is now a Level 4 FasterEFT practitioner and finds FasterEFT to be his preferred modality with clients. René offers FasterEFT seminars and sessions in both French and Spanish.

Websites:

French-Language

www.zenrilla.be

Spanish-Language

www.fastereftlatino.com

YouTube:

Zenrilla

From Mr. Mom to Global Stress Expert

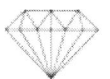

Robert Smith

I was born and grew up in Oklahoma. Before FasterEFT, my life looked like it was never going to go anywhere. In 1999, I was a stay-at-home dad with three kids, living in a mobile home and with no income of my own. My wife had a job, and I was "Mr. Mom". I would try to help make ends meet by working on cars. I never thought I could drive anything newer than a 1978 because I wouldn't be able to fix it. I had grease under my fingernails, calluses on my hands, and big issues in my marriage.

At that stage, I didn't believe that I could ever have anything better – that was how life was always going to be.

My upbringing hadn't set me up for much more in life than I had achieved by 1999. My step-father (the only father I've known) was uneducated, hard-working and angry. I didn't like myself, and was carrying a lot of anger, hurt and emotional pain. I was short-tempered and sensitive, with a belief that I wasn't very intelligent and would never be good enough. At that stage, I didn't believe that I could ever have anything better – that was how life was always going to be.

There were issues in my relationship with my wife that I believed were connected to the trauma she'd experience in her past – the stuff she didn't even want to look at let alone deal with. I figured that the answer to fixing our relationship was fixing her. Of course, it doesn't work that way, and what I didn't recognize at the time was that I had just as many problems as she had. But, finding someone that could help her opened the door for us both to start healing.

I had already learned NLP – listening to Anthony Robins' tapes and applying the process, using it on myself. I was always listening to self-help stuff. Now, I went even further into NLP, and we found a therapist who taught it. One of his students pointed me in the direction of EFT. I bought the EFT course; and, after letting it sit around for a bit, I decided to watch the videos and read the book. Then, I started using it.

I would tap on anything that moved!
Eventually, over time, it developed into the FasterEFT process we have today.

Things began to change. And as I continued using a combination of EFT and NLP, I started to add in elements from other modalities, including Be Set Free Fast, Touch and Breathe, and hypnosis. The more I learned about the way the mind works, the more I developed the technique I was using. I kept changing it and adjusting it to address different problems more effectively as I worked on other people as well as myself. I would tap on anything that moved! Eventually, over time, it developed into the FasterEFT process we have today.

As I've developed FasterEFT, and continued to use it on myself, my life has completely changed. I see myself completely differently now. I no longer have the anger issues – in fact, my reaction to people today has completely changed. My life now is like someone else's life. Back in 1999, I couldn't have even imagined this lifestyle.

I am proud of the work I do and the way I am; and I now know that I'm a good person.
My life is better and more fulfilling than I could ever have imagined! And it's because I did the work on myself.

Now, instead of living in a mobile home, hustling, working on old cars and trying to make ends meet, I'm travelling the world, giving seminars and helping hundreds of thousands of people through my YouTube videos. Instead of being filled with self-loathing, I am proud of the work I do and the way I am; and I now know that I'm a good person. I am surrounded by people who love me and care for me. I get emails from people all over the world, telling me how FasterEFT has changed their lives. My life is better and more fulfilling than I could ever have imagined! And it's because I did the work on myself.

There was some big stuff inside me. I remember the biggest, nastiest, scariest thing inside me. And I was afraid to go there; but I still looked at it, and still tapped on it. The biggest reason I have got to where I am today from where I was, is persistence. And that's the most important advice I can give to anyone who wants to transform their life – be persistent. It might not happen in one session. It might take longer than you expect, but keep going until you get what you want. And you'll see changes along the way too.

Now, because of the work I've done on myself, and because I've been using FasterEFT for so long, when something happens in my life, I don't necessarily need to tap. I can mentally process it, and I don't have to physically tap because I let it go mentally. My mind understands it, and we work as a team now. Now, that doesn't mean I don't have problems. Everyone has problems, that's life. And sometimes I do need to tap. But the problems are not overwhelming anymore. I have the tools and the skills to handle them. I will never end up back in the same place I used to be, because I'm a completely different person now. So, anything that comes up for me now, I will experience it differently. I can handle it. I'm happy now.

My passion is helping people, and I'm doing what I love every day.

Robert is the creator of FasterEFT and CEO of Skills to Change Institute Inc. He conducts workshops, and training seminars internationally, and has been a seeker of truth for the last 40 years. He has a passion for what actually works ... it must be logical and practical. He then shares what he's learned with the world. Robert also volunteers his time in drug treatment centers and abuse centers, and gives to others in so many ways.

Website:

www.fastereft.com

can you Believe it !

Facebook:

www.facebook.com/groups/fastereft

YouTube:

www.youtube.com/user/HealingMagic

A Nurse's Recovery

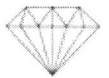

Rose Hargrove

This is the story of my journey from healing to illness, and of emerging from illness into a new life.

This part of my story starts after high school. When I started college I wanted nothing more than to become a nurse. In the days when I was in nursing school, students were seen as a source of labor, and my earliest experience in nursing was to witness a disaster.

As a young nursing student, after a tornado had devastated a nearby town, I was loaded onto a bus with my fellow classmates and we were driven into that town to help in any way we could. I have never seen anything like what greeted us when we got off the bus. Houses were splintered, and cars were standing up on end. I won't continue with the description other than to say it left its mark on my heart. I had learned my primary lesson - that nurses were there to help and that we could do anything if we just persevered.

In nursing school, I attained the dean's list, and, except for a few courses that weren't related to my career, I did very well. Upon graduating I took my boards and passed them.

Freshly out of school, I applied for a position at a local hospital in the operating room. That's a pretty ambitious move for a new graduate, but I was very certain of myself. Not long after starting my job, I saw the somber reality of the work I was doing.

When you're a student, you are shielded from the more graphic aspects of nursing. After six months in surgical work, I had come to the decision that I needed experience in a different area and that I needed a less stressful situation. The next job I accepted was in the emergency room. I now wonder how much less stressful that position was! But it was a different place and it didn't run at the same speed as the surgical unit did, which I saw as something positive.

After a year of very intense work, I took a break and worked in the clinic for a while, and there I studied advanced cardiac life support and discovered I was developing asthma that was rather debilitating. I started taking injections to desensitize myself to my allergens - but the injections didn't seem to help very much, and I was using inhalers and injections to manage. Then I found Dr. Stanislav Grof and Holotropic Breathwork. I was drawn to this new therapy and the transformational aspects. My asthma was eventually relieved, however my thoughts and beliefs were essentially the same.

I continued to work in my chosen profession but decided to leave medical nursing for psychiatric nursing. By doing so, I thought I would be leaving the more graphic part of medical practice behind. I worked at the Veterans Administration hospital, and there I was trained in PTSD treatment and worked with severely addicted veterans, former prisoners of war, and the chronically mentally ill. It became apparent that there was a great deal of trauma to go around.

Eventually I found myself working in a civilian hospital in charge of night duty in the psychiatric emergency department. I oversaw six emergency rooms, dispatching on-call people and evaluating patients in my own emergency room.

I was working when the Columbine shooting occurred and was very certain that I had not seen such sadness in my life. Before that point, my health had started to decline, but it was unclear what was wrong. I saw multiple doctors with no clear answer. I finally talked to an emergency room doctor who is a friend of mine and asked him if he knew of any physician who could give me an answer. He said he did, but that the doctor was extremely busy and it would take some time before I could get in to see him. Nonetheless I made an appointment. When I did finally see this respected doctor, he told me that I needed to consult a specialist in rheumatology. I asked him what he thought my problem was, and he said that I had something much more serious than arthritis, and he feared that it was lupus.

I was willing to do anything to find an answer.

I saw a rheumatologist, and she couldn't make up her mind between two equally devastating diagnoses. I was frightened and put off by her manner, so I told the first doctor I couldn't go back to this rheumatologist. He suggested another rheumatologist who was much kinder and possibly more thorough. The second rheumatologist didn't have much difficulty making the diagnosis. He said that I had systemic lupus and that I needed to be started on immunosuppressants to preserve my systems. I didn't argue with him as the pain was becoming intolerable, and I was willing to do anything to find an answer. Eventually the difficulties that the lupus posed cost me my job, and I found myself to be another disabled person looking for an answer and praying that I would live.

Soon various medical procedures were started, and the lupus became more threatening. I had taken pride in keeping up my health even after the diagnosis, but now my teeth were failing me and eventually I lifted an object that wasn't very heavy, yet my spine fractured.

My doctor had me rushed into surgery in the next few days and the first of two repairs was done. The second repair took five hours and left me with nerve pressure at the base of my spine and worsening migraines. Then the focal seizures started to show up, so my doctor sent me to see two neurologists, but neither man could come up with an answer.

They tried various medications, eventually giving me time-release morphine so that I could rest. Later a CT angiogram of my brain was done, and still no one could come to an answer. During that angiogram, I went into shock. I was tended to and stabilized, but on the way home after that procedure, I decided I didn't have much of a future.

Later that day, while my son and I were eating lunch, I thought about it and knew that I had to find an answer. I sought out various emotional healing modalities, including NLP. These were all helpful but were not the complete answer. I needed to confront my thoughts and my beliefs.

Eventually, I found out about FasterEFT, and I started working with first a Level 1 and then a Level 2 practitioner. I started to see some progress but needed something more. The Level 2 practitioner told me that if I were to work with Robert Smith, the creator of FasterEFT, perhaps I would see some results. I looked at what the tuition cost and told her I didn't have it - but right at that time Robert was offering to allow people with lupus into his class without charge.

I talked to the other women in my lupus support group about my discovery of FasterEFT, and they had no interest and thought that I was silly for even taking part in it. Didn't I realize that they were doing research and the cure for lupus was just around the corner? I didn't hold out much hope for the research.

I really couldn't afford to fly to where the class was in Las Vegas, and I couldn't afford a hotel. I was living on disability. I started a 'go fund me' campaign, started tapping with some people online, and came across a man named Fritz. The first time I conversed with him, he asked me was I a nurse and did I work in psychiatry. I said I used to, and he said he was a retired physician. I started to realize that this man was very, very intelligent, and I asked him what his specialty was in medicine. He replied psychiatry. I had met someone who was to become one of my best friends and FasterEFT mentors. Fritz helped me financially and, even more, helped me understand what I needed to do to heal myself.

Was there something in my brain that had been changed?

I did go to the FasterEFT Level 1 training and shared a room with a woman who had to wheel me in a wheelchair to the class because I was still

ill. Being at the training brought out all of my stressors and traumas. Although I didn't quite understand it at the time, the stressors and traumas were there to be looked at and let go. During the training, I met and spoke with Robert Smith and Deirdre Maguire. Robert told me that I needed to focus on the painful parts of my relationships in life, especially with my mother. I cried and cried for most of my time there.

Robert offered for me to have a crossfire session with two FasterEFT practitioners who could possibly help me find my answers. I remember going to the session and meeting Kim Jewell and Laura Worley. They were marvellous and helped me find the areas that I needed to let go of. When I left the session I was sort of confused and didn't know quite what to make of all of it. Was there something in my brain that had been changed?

I was in complete remission from lupus!

When I returned home, I continued to meet with other practitioners online as I had completed Level 1 and wanted more practice with the technique. I went on to the Level 2 training, where I met Fritz in person. He asked me to repeat Level 1, which I did. While I was sitting there in that Level 1 training class, my phone buzzed and buzzed. It was my doctor in Denver. I had seen him prior to leaving, when he examined me, told me I was looking better, and ordered bloodwork. During that phone call while I was in FasterEFT training, my doctor said my bloodwork was back and that he couldn't find any more signs of lupus in my blood or in my physical exam. I was in complete remission from lupus! I was very excited. I told Fritz, and then I told Robert . It was such a shock that I didn't know what to make of it.

I then went on to Level 3 training and met Kim and Dave Ryder. Through talking with them I came to realize how I became ill. I wasn't alone, and many other nurses were in the same position. In fact, I knew four nurses who had lupus. It was then that my nurse trauma program was born. I am still a nurse, but my new career focus is to help other nurses find their answers, just as I have found mine.

FasterEFT has helped me to change my thoughts away from darkness and sickness to start a new life. Now that I am so much better, I want to help others achieve the same. I'm very thankful for all those who helped me along my journey, and I'm very thankful for FasterEFT.

Rose Hargrove, RN, is originally from Rockford, Illinois, in the United States. She attended nursing school at Rock Valley College and then respiratory therapy school at both Swedish American Hospital and the University of Chicago.

Rose worked for half of her career in acute care and then opted to follow another path, in the mental health field. She took training in PTSD therapy through the Veterans Administration Medical Center (VAMC) and then went on to be trained as an addiction counselor, for which she is certified in both Illinois and Colorado. After a divorce, Rose relocated to Denver with her two young children to accept a position at that city's VAMC. She found this experience to be somewhat scary, yet very exciting.

A few years later Rose left the veterans hospital and found a position in a civilian hospital working in the psychiatric emergency department. Soon, she was moved to the night shift and was overseeing psychiatric emergencies for six hospitals. It was then she realized that her 'adventures in healthcare' had resulted in her own illness. She proceeded to investigate alternative therapies when allopathic medicine no longer held any answers for her. After studying various modalities, she experienced the most pronounced healing results with FasterEFT and became a Level 3 practitioner.

Rose's new path is healing and life-affirming. With the help of emotional modalities, she has developed a blog and a program to help other nurses deal with the stresses and traumas that often occur in a healthcare career. The primary focus is FasterEFT, where she has seen many people find real transformation and lasting results.

Rose looks forward to meeting you and helping you to find lasting wellness.

Website:

www.rosehargrove.com

Nursing Blog:

www.findingwellnessinnursing.wordpress.com

I Learned to Ask for Help

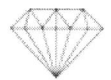

Rosita Kingston

> Tapping for me now is like breathing - automatic.

A decade since first discovering FasterEFT, tapping for me now is like breathing - automatic. It's my first response to any upset within me or around me. I don't think about doing it, I just do it – in the same way we don't consciously think: 'I need to breathe.' It's involuntary.

> Tapping with FasterEFT is one good habit
> which I am glad I've developed.

When you tap consistently about everything that bothers you, it becomes a habit. I'm tapping now about writing this piece, because of the resistance it brings up in me - insecurities about self-expression, not doing it perfectly, avoiding getting down to it, yadda, yadda, yadda. 'Old tapes' sometimes still run in my head. Yes, I still have a few bad habits, but tapping with FasterEFT is one good habit which I am glad I've developed.

There is a peculiar phenomenon which will be very familiar to practitioners of FasterEFT. When we work with someone to clear up a problem, it's often followed by complete amnesia. The thing that weighed on them so heavily and bothered them so much will be so totally GONE! It's as though it were never there at all. They find it hard to believe it was ever that bad. I myself have experienced this so often in my own life that now, having to recall how I was (pre-FasterEFT) for the purposes of this story, it's actually a difficult exercise for me.

We catch ourselves responding very differently.

The other thing is, the changes we experience are gradual and often very subtle, so that we may not even be aware of the shifts we have made. Often we only realise we've changed because someone close to us brings it to our attention or we may find ourselves in a particular situation which previously would have triggered us, and we catch ourselves responding very differently. I can see clearly the changes in Ken, my husband, for instance. Angst has been replaced by ease, and it's a natural ease, not a white-knuckled efforting.

Just couldn't get life 'right.'

Ken and I have been together a long time. We were both 'searchers' from a young age, and together we have been great teachers for one another. Since my early 20s, I travelled down many avenues looking for answers to the problems my life presented. They were the usual problems, you could say – family-of-origin stuff, things in my past which I just wanted to bury and forget about (but couldn't), unhealthy patterns in relationships, feelings of inadequacy, and powerlessness over certain aspects of my life. As a practitioner of FasterEFT, I have come to know that we all have basically the same 'stuff' within us. In my case, for instance, it's been neatly underpinned by a deep self-criticism that I, Rosita Kingston, just couldn't get life 'right.'

I wanted that inner peace, that balance.

My best coping skill was to try to stay in control and to strive for perfection.

If everything looked okay, then perhaps it would be okay. But let's just say that the inside didn't match the outside – and, really, even though I probably wouldn't have been able to name it, that's what I was looking for. I wanted that inner peace, that balance. To feel good about life and good about myself (most of the time) is what I wanted - and it seemed I'd never find it.

I read A LOT of self-help books, attended 12-step groups, went to counseling, and even did primal therapy. And yes, I gained something valuable from all of these. But the searching went on so long, I began to believe it would never end. I was stuck with my crap - stuck with those behavior patterns which I knew were obsolete, but which I felt powerless to change.

We had the same argument about the same stuff!

Here I was in a long-term, fulfilling relationship with a similarly gifted artist and kindred spirit, yet any time we argued, it was like a tape playing – we had the same argument about the same stuff! Relationship - intimate, long-term, functional relationship is difficult to carve out. For Ken and I, thankfully, the partnership, fun, joy part of us together always outweighs the discord. And we were all the time learning and growing from our own self-development pursuits.

And then we became parents.

I was 29 years old having our first child together.

We called her Lucy. She was born in the little maternity 'house' at Belfast City Hospital on a Sunday morning, June 30th 1996. An auburn-haired ray of sunshine.

> The world shifted on its axis.
> Our lives were turned upside down.

We took her home to a sweet house in the suburbs we'd bought and decorated together. She was a shining child. We loved her so much. We had so much fun with her. She was an easy child to parent, and so bright! She reached all those baby milestones well ahead of time – except the toddling/walking milestone, which we weren't concerned about really, in the beginning. But at age 18 months and still not getting around on her own, we took Lucy for some tests. She had Spinal Muscular Atrophy, a neuromuscular disorder which affects the transmission of messages from the brain to the muscles, so they don't work. Atrophy means waste away.

Lucy would never walk.

The world shifted on its axis. Our lives were turned upside down.

Still, we went on the trip to the U.S. that we'd planned. Lucy turned 2 in New York, and then we went on to Seattle for a month – and that is how we proceeded. We lived our lives and raised our child. In the process, I was forced to give up on the perfection illusion. Our little girl wasn't perfect. She was flawed genetically and there was nothing we could do about it.

I learned to ask for help.

I learned to ask for help. That was a difficult one – admitting that I couldn't 'do it all.' I come eighth in a family of eleven, and my mom DID do it all. I believed it was possible. In fact, I believed it was my duty. Letting go of that belief took a long time. Lucy taught me SO much.

I became an advocate for her with a degree of tenacity I never knew was in me, making sure she had what she needed when she needed it. Before she was 3, Lucy was driving her own miniature, powered wheelchair! I developed biceps like Madonna, from carrying her. Ken used to carry Lucy and dance around to music - even when she was much older. What a workout that was! She loved that.

Lucy wasn't able to move in her sleep, as we all do. One of us turned her in the night (at least once) every night. There were a few periods of illness. People with Spinal Muscular Atrophy get chest infections easily, but she was basically a healthy child - attending school, interested in many things, gifted artistically - and with a wisdom well beyond her years.

We outgrew Belfast and made the move to Port Townsend, Washington, (in the U.S.) the summer Lucy was 5. I was pregnant, and Lucy's earnest wish for a baby sister was granted when Ruby was born the following spring. Another redheaded beauty!

It was a time of new beginnings and real joy, but at the same time, it became a major turning point in the relationship between Ken and I.

'Get strong or go under'

All those hairline cracks in our partnership, which previously we'd successfully circumnavigated, were now being busted wide open. Things between us got really bad. We'd have split up – we tried, but our circumstances just wouldn't allow it. For me, personally, it was a case of 'get strong or go under' – and get strong I did, through my weekly codependence anonymous group, the friendships I'd developed with women around me, and a 'guardian angel' counsellor I found.

We limped through the winter of 2002, spending that Christmas in hospital with Lucy. At some point in the New Year we surrendered. Looking at one another across the room, our next move was obvious to us both: we needed family support. So we set about returning to Ireland - this time to County Cork, where I'm from and where the concentration of family is.

Lucy was 7 and Ruby 18 months. We settled in Kinsale, found a wheelchair-friendly home, bought a vehicle, enrolled Lucy in the local school with her cousins, and opened a studio/art school in the next town. So began another chapter. And this was the chapter when FasterEFT came into our lives.

Lucy's spine curved dramatically as she grew. She became less able to do things she was previously able to do with ease. She was being sorely challenged, and anxiety took hold of her. She seemed to internalize her worries and fears, which began to be expressed as bouts of cyclical vomiting, usually preceded by a headache. Then she'd need to be admitted to hospital for re-hydration. Either Ken or I always stayed with her. Hospital stays became more frequent for Lucy, now aged 9.

It's often through sheer desperation, when our 'backs are against the wall,' that we find the tapping. We were in that place.

We were worn out, desperate to help our child and to regain some kind of a family life. I know many of you will understand what I mean when I say that it's often through sheer desperation, when our 'backs are against the wall,' that we find the tapping. We were in that place.

Discovering that anxiety was at the root of Lucy's bouts of illness, Ken found EFT (emotional freedom technique) online when he typed in the word 'anxiety' and ran a search.

So we started tapping - on Lucy, and on ourselves. And it helped - a lot. At last we had a tool that we could use. And use it we did - although in the beginning all we knew was the longer, traditional EFT method.

I tapped to stay sane.

I knew this much: that I was no good to Lucy as a despairing, worried parent. I tapped to maintain some degree of equilibrium - to stay sane. Ken did likewise. We both knew how important it was.

On the morning of December 8th, she died.
In her own bed, with Ken tapping on her as she left us.

Lucy was hospitalized again in November 2006. She was failing so dramatically, physically. Bed was the only comfortable place. Then, on the morning of December 8th, she died. In her own bed, with Ken tapping on her as she left us.

Because I tapped, I was able to survive.

Because I tapped, I was able to speak, without breaking down, at Lucy's funeral service. I was able to honour her with my words, something which I am so grateful for.

Because I tapped, I was able to survive.

Because I tapped, I was able to function as a fully present mother to Ruby, still only 4 years old.

Then we found FasterEFT, developed by Robert Smith, and it allowed me to not just survive but to thrive. Ken and I consumed the YouTube videos, learning all we could, and then worked with Robert via Skype. We shared our skills helping others with everything from chocolate addiction to exam stress, and of course grief and loss. Wanting the world to know of this tool for transformation, we welcomed Robert to Kinsale in 2009, where he gave a talk to a capacity audience - and began a love affair with Ireland resulting in many more teaching visits, North and South. We also went on to train with him in Oklahoma.

I am not exaggerating when I say
FasterEFT saved our lives.
If you feel lousy and tap, you're owning your feelings as yours and doing something about it. No blame.

I am not exaggerating when I say FasterEFT saved our lives. It saved our sanity, our relationship, and our family unit. We found that when you tap, you quit pointing the finger at anyone else as the source of your problem. If you feel lousy and tap, you're owning your feelings as yours and doing something about it. No blame.

We learned SO Much at the trainings and seminars – and ALL OF IT made sense.

> 'This is it. I can call off the search.'

I remember at some point telling Ken, 'This is it. I can call off the search,' and feeling a deep sense of gratitude – and *relief*, because I had honestly thought I would never be able to say that.

> That, my friend is a gift. I am honoured that I get to pass it on.

I tapped to let go of guilt I felt around Lucy's death. I was even able to change awful memories of Lucy's sickness, so that the happy memory of her helping me in the kitchen is the one that comes to my mind first. I came to really know that Lucy is free, not convince myself, but really know in my heart and accept that 10-and-a-half years was her lifespan and be okay with that. That, my friend is a gift. And I am so grateful Robert Smith shared the gift of FasterEFT with the world, and I am honoured that I get to pass it on.

Ken and I work with clients individually and together and give free talks about FasterEFT.

> There is a harmony and an ease between us today.
>
> I forgive me.

We long ago ceased to have the 'same argument' scenario. There is a harmony and an ease between us today which we are both so thankful for. Ruby is 14 now. Tapping with FasterEFT helps me keep my perspective as the mother of a fiery teenager. I no longer consume self-help books or latch on to the latest anything.

FasterEFT has taught me that I have the power within me and the sole responsibility for my life. And the more I tap and let go of what I don't want, the more my life opens up naturally. And yes, sometimes I opt to 'sit in the mess' rather than doing anything about it, and yes, I'm impatient and frustrated with my seemingly slow progress at times. I'm a flawed human being – but I accept ME more. I'm more compassionate to myself. I forgive me.

Of course we continue to be challenged. That is the nature of life. We've just completed another house move – our fourth move in 7 years. But when FasterEFT tapping is as natural as breathing, it's okay. I'm okay. I'm feeling good about life and good about myself most of the time.

Thank you, Lucy. Thank you, Robert.

Rosita studied Art originally & now combines Art and FasterEFT, together with other healing modalities, to help herself and others towards self-actualization. She has plans to begin blogging, and speaking publicly more.

Email:

theartofpositivechange@gmail.com

I Was Born to be Doing This Work

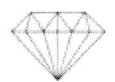

Sarah Batsanis

Before FasterEFT, I was searching for meaning to life.

I felt powerless. I felt such a mess, like it was all just too much!

I felt lost, lonely, unloved, and unimportant. I was blaming the world (and my partner) for my problems and how I was feeling. I felt powerless. I was looking for a way to find myself - as well as how to overcome the stress, heartache, and built-up resentment from my relationship. I thought it was my job to deal with my issues myself, and soldier on. I wasn't even sure that anyone, or anything, could help. I felt such a mess, like it was all just too much! I felt sure no one would understand me.

I had been watching a local TV station here in Australia, and saw a lady using a 'tapping' technique for her cravings to fast food, specifically fried chicken. It wasn't until a few years later that I would notice in my local paper an ad – also about 'tapping.' It started out, 'Do you suffer from . . . ?' and gave a whole list of different symptoms that could be addressed. I quickly made the phone call and booked in for a session. I then discovered that Robert Smith, the creator of a tapping modality called FasterEFT, would be coming to Australia to train practitioners for Level 1 of his system. I decided to attend.

For the most part, I was very skeptical.
My stubbornness didn't want to believe that something so simple could be so profound - but boy was I wrong!

Truthfully, for the most part, I was very skeptical. Being quite a logical person, it took me 6 months even after my FasterEFT training before I would use the tapping on an ongoing basis. My stubbornness and ego didn't want to believe that something so simple could be so profound - but boy was I wrong! Looking back, I know now that I could have found peace a lot sooner if I'd known of tapping and had started putting it into practice in my daily life.

My experience of FasterEFT was amazing. I was surprised by the fast results, and even though I didn't know how it all worked, the funny thing was, it still worked! The things that had once bothered me, I could no longer get annoyed about.

The changes were amazing! After just a few sessions, my outlook on life was different. My health improved, my back pain and stomach pain cleared up, I was more calm and relaxed than ever before, and I was able to have a much more loving relationship with my partner and children. My self-esteem went up too. I felt more confident, and was able to take my power back from past events. I now had more control over my emotions and my life.

I was amazed by the results - so much so that even my addiction to chocolate was cleared up too. I was no longer in the cupboard every night looking for sweets. And guess what? We didn't even work on the addiction directly! ☺

It was an unexpected bonus I received through tapping out and releasing my built-up stress and emotions - now that they were no longer hidden within me!

My life now is one of bliss, unconditional love, freedom, and peace. I have come to a beautiful space of ease and flow, and enjoy living each day as if it's my last.

I am free to be me. I found myself, and I love who I am.

I now feel blessed to do the work that I love, and get to teach and coach these wonderful FasterEFT learnings and techniques to both my children and clients. I live my truth, and I express myself without the worry of what others think. I am free to be me. I found myself, and I love who I am. I also enjoy helping others to find themselves, and love who they are - as well as have happier, more heartfelt relationships.

I was born to be doing this work.

My daughter once said to me, 'Mum, if you weren't doing FasterEFT, what else would you be doing instead?' I paused. I thought long and hard, and I then turned to her and said. 'Nothing! There is nothing else I'd rather be doing than using FasterEFT to help people to free themselves. I was born to be doing this work.'

Sarah Batsanis is one of Australia's leading stress specialists and relationship mentors. She is a Love & Confidence Coach and speaker and is passionate about creating lasting positive change in people.

Sarah has been working with relationships and giving people the life-empowering skills to quickly help change how they feel and live so they can express their highest truth, find love, and make connections.

Her work has helped people gain understanding within themselves, as well as clarity and peace of mind when it comes to personal and romantic relationships.

Some of Sarah's main areas of focus are helping people find love, fix broken relationships, gain confidence, and stop stress. She works with her clients primarily using FasterEFT, a cutting edge system that works to address unwanted emotions and physical pain within the mind and body.

Website:
www.fastereft.com.au

Email:
sarah@fastereft.com.au

can you Believe it !

Facebook:

www.facebook.com/fastereftaustralia/

Sarah is also a contributor at:

www.inspirationbible.com

can you Believe it !

Heal Me or Kill Me, God

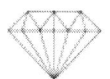

Suzan Vaughn

The story I'm telling here is part of my journey back to wellness.

I had given up on my hopes, dreams, and future.

By 2009, life had lost most of its meaning for me. I felt I had officially 'lost the plot.' I had been in college, finishing my degree in psychology, when the insomnia started, and pain began ripping through me. It was more than I could bear, and I was forced to resign from school after years of study. I had given up on my hopes, dreams, and future.

I couldn't be touched without pain, movement was difficult, and I 'knew' that if I physically exerted myself, I would pay dearly.

In 2004, after consulting more physicians than I can recall, I was diagnosed with fibromyalgia and depression by a leading expert in Dallas, Texas. I had 15 of the 18 trigger points needed to make the diagnosis. I couldn't be touched without pain, movement was difficult, and I 'knew' that if I physically exerted myself, I would pay dearly.

Time seemed to stop as I began to willfully waste away. I was rendered irresponsible by my own body. 'Why me?' was often a part of my thoughts. I further lost control by addictions to prescription painkillers Percocet, OxyContin, and Xanax, as I reached for anything I could use to cope.

>When joy did come, I seemed to refuse it.
>I recall asking God to either 'heal me or kill me' on several occasions.

When joy did come, I seemed to refuse it. I thought I didn't deserve to feel good and I felt there was 'proof' of that inside me. In an attempt to escape my reality, I ran from all the physical and emotional pain that had been haunting me for more than two decades. Every day was a struggle. I felt completely broken and prayed for release. I recall asking God to either 'heal me or kill me' on several occasions. I even tried to commit suicide.

Looking back, this potential 'escape' was the only thing I felt I could control until the day came that even that was no longer controllable. There was nothing, not one aspect, left in my control. Rather, the pain and disease controlled me. What else could I do to cope? I subscribed to all of the powerlessness groups bearing sympathy and tried to cope that way. On top of everything else, I was addicted now. I was armed with bottles of pills, about 12 different prescriptions, to relieve the pain that grew only stronger as I kept searching for a solution.

>Help was on the way in a most extraordinary way.

What I didn't know was that I had a choice. Just like the coping mechanisms I utilized, I could be in control of my own healing too. I didn't have to accept the path that I created. I didn't have to take those doctors' words as the gospel and make them true within me. It wasn't too late! I could believe something different. Help was on the way in a most extraordinary way.

I had been trying to find the answer at the bottom of those prescription bottles. Looking back, I recall my husband telling me to stop looking, as there was no cure. He, along with each professional, told me that the best I could hope for was to find a way to manage my disease. A part of me knew that life could be better - but for every empowering thought I had there was that little contradicting voice that said, 'There isn't a cure' or 'Give up, already.' Well-meaning doctors and relatives reinforced my self-victimization and completely supported the downward spiral of any well-being I had left. As months turned into years, I played that role very well.

When you are ill, you'll hear questions and comments that continue to support the beliefs you have about yourself, like . . .
'Are you ok?'
'Let me get that for you.'
'Are you sure you can do that?'
'What about the pain?' and *'Is there anything I can do for you?'*

We are all supposed to be empathetic, right?

You'll also hear statements, like, 'I hope you feel better,' or 'Be careful!' - not to mention, the grimacing looks on the faces of others as they see you struggle. After all, we are all supposed to be empathetic, right?

Our pain is a representation of our emotional state.
It is real, and it has a message.

You get the picture. Just like me, you are a product of beliefs that either serve you or don't. Those beliefs are keeping you in alignment with what you hold within yourself, and all this is motivated by love, all to keep you 'safe.' Our pain is a representation of our emotional state. It is real, and it has a message.

I found this truth in FasterEFT.

Little did I know, it is the job of the subconscious mind – to keep me safe. But oddly enough, I found that 'what I resisted, persisted.' My body was telling me loud and clear, 'Listen to me!' I couldn't run far enough, fast enough. I would never succeed in finding the answer at the bottom of a bottle, in another person, or through my co-dependency of both. I didn't realize that if I dealt with (and even embraced) the parts of myself that were hurting, I would not only heal, I could help others to do the same.
I found this truth in FasterEFT.

It was my season to heal and I knew it.

In the beginning of 2010, I found the 'Healing Magic' channel on YouTube. It contained videos posted by Robert Smith, the founder of FasterEFT. I began tapping along with many, many of the videos, as if I was sitting in that chair, with Robert tapping on me. It was my season to heal and I knew it. This belief only grew as I watched and learned more about how I was doing this to myself, within myself.

I began feeding the information to my subconscious by repeating the words said in the videos, and tapping along. For six months, I did this - until there came a day where I found myself doing things I hadn't done in years and enjoying life! It sounds a bit strange, but I will never forget one particular morning I stood at my kitchen sink, doing dishes, for the first time in a long time. All I could do was thank God for answering my prayer by allowing me to find this modality.

'Told patient to keep doing whatever she is doing.'

At first, resistance reared up in defense of what was under the surface. But letting go of limiting beliefs, I kept going. That became my mantra, 'Just keep going.' I eventually decided that it was the time to take even more action and agreed to see Robert in person. For three days he tapped with me, and although there was so much work to do, I knew I had found what I'd been searching for and continued healing myself.

My journals of self-work accumulated, and the day came when my physician wrote in my chart: 'Told patient to keep doing whatever she is doing.' I would successfully be taken off all nine medications prescribed for pain management, anxiety, insomnia, and depression, and tell-tale symptoms of fibromyalgia.

I was successfully creating my pain, based on the life I had lived thus far.

THIS IS THE THING . . . .

The terms, labels, and name tags I had grown to use (such as, addiction and fibromyalgia) were the physical manifestation of all that stuff in the past that I had never chosen to resolve or let go. I was successfully creating my pain, based on the life I had lived thus far. I was truly doing it to myself in the 'now.' Those things weren't happening any longer, yet my body and mind were trying to protect me in the most loving of ways and trying to keep me safe by doing the same things they'd always done. And that is what had resulted in illness. My past had taken control and manifested through pain and denial.

Some of the darkest places held the healing resources I needed for growth.

I felt that I deserved a respite from the pain through those medications. Yet true relief came only when I began to go of all those traumatic experiences, to fully feel them without running, to release them, and to completely transform them. With memory after memory, I began healing those hurts, finding the courage to relive them in order to feel the pain for the last time. Some of the darkest places held the healing resources I needed for growth.

No longer were they trying to run the show. I had taken control of my own life!

My deepest desire is to help others and to enjoy each and every moment. I am thankful for the opportunities afforded to me.

I sleep easily and in peace each night.

I believe that inside each of us is unlimited potential for miraculous change. You came into this world, a divine spark, and only you have the power to allow growth in your life. My own life continues to unfold in the most beautiful ways. Watching others change and let go of their story is a privilege in this lifetime. My clients are becoming happier and healthier. I sleep easily and in peace each night.

I found this to be true: FasterEFT is a powerful system that can be used on any problem, issue, pain, or symptom - and it can put you back in the driver's seat of your own life. Isn't it time to take your power back and create the life you are meant to live?

There is so much goodness in life. Choose happiness! The choice really is yours.

Suzan Vaughn, a Level 3 FasterEFT practitioner at Your Time To Heal, *lives in McKinney, Texas, in the United States with her husband and daughter. Since 2013, her mission has been to empower and educate others through the use of FasterEFT. She is also skilled and certified in hypnosis and Neuro Linguistic Programming (NLP), among other modalities.*

Suzan believes that life is to be enjoyed and doesn't take it so seriously. She knows that the body has a natural ability to heal itself, if given the right care. She has healed herself of addiction, depression, and fibromyalgia.

Suzan is dedicated to helping people – not just in her community, but also worldwide - who truly want a better life for themselves and their families. Her goal is to open your eyes and show you how extraordinary and valuable you really are to this planet. She continues to pursue education that will serve her clients and trains on a regular basis. She is in private practice and provides 30-minute initial consultations at no cost.

Website:

www.yourtimetoheal.com

Email:

suzan@yourtimetoheal.com

Telephone:

(+1) 469-254-8314

Time Zone:

http://www.timeanddate.com/worldclock/usa/dallas

Conclusion

Why you could read this book again
and again …

"A good story is hard to beat."

That's what I learned, growing up. In the ancient annals of Irish culture there was no better man than the 'seanachai' (the story-teller). A country emaciated by the poverty of famine and war, our culture procured its nourishment from language. The abundance of Prolific Irish writers is a testimony to this.

It turns out there is **science** in the 'Success of the Story', the 'Power of the Parable'. Not only is storytelling fundamental to our way of life, it's common to every culture. In Jonathan Gottschall's book, "The Storytelling Animal," he says, "the constant firing of our neurons in response to stimuli strengthens and refines the neural pathways that lead to skilful navigation of life's problems".

So why are these transformational life records so powerful? Because they demonstrate two essential core components of mind/body science:

1. **We model our behaviour (from each other.)**

The baby duck that thinks it's a hen.
 i.e. **If they can do, it we can do it too.**

2. **What we believe to be true, is true for us.**

(Remember when you believed in Santa, the Tooth Fairy, cartoon characters?)

i.e. **One's truth is the most powerful tool of all.**

The personal reality accounts in this book, although widely varied, have two common threads: The real life experience of powerful courage in the face of adversity; and the live demonstration of the system that served the changes being made. That's what makes them at least as (if not more) powerful than any book about the theory of FasterEFT.

Science tells us today that **what you believe is more important than what's true,** and so I invite you to get clever! Use these stories to get your own momentum going! Tidy up any limiting beliefs that you have picked up. Let FasterEFT help you to improve the quality of your own life story **and** reach wherever you want to be!

Because:

You are just as heroic as the people in this book.

The question is:

Can you Believe it ! ...

can you Believe it !

What's the Next Step?

A typical response from people who meet me for the first time is: "You're very passionate about your work aren't you?"

The truth is, I want more and more people to know there is a better way to live! The transformations I have the privilege to witness every day in my one-to-one sessions is my proof that this is possible.

So maybe you can help me .

Are you ready to share your story?

If so, we want to hear it. Here are some guidelines to help you. Make your story an inspiration to others.
You will be credited for your submission, or you can remain anonymous, if you prefer.

1. What was your life like before FasterEFT? (i.e. the unmanageability of it, etc.) (250 words)

2. What else have you tried? (100 words)

3. How did you come to find FasterEFT? (100 words)

4. What were your expectations, fears, doubts, scepticisms? (100 words)

5. What was your experience of FasterEFT like? (250 words)

6. What changes did you experience afterward? (200-400 words)

7. How is your life today? (200 words)

can you Believe it ! II and **can you Believe it ! - A Solution to Addiction** are both on their way.

My plan is to donate these books to shelters, prisons, schools, rehabilitation units, and other charities. If you would like to suggest a charity please email us at: canyoubelieveit@deirdremaguire.com

If you would like to contribute, go to www.deirdremaguire.com donate button. For every £15 you donate we will send 2 copies of **can you Believe it !** to a charity. We will acknowledge receipt of your donation and let you know where the books you paid for were sent.

The truth for me is that:

We are all Ordinary People
with Extraordinary Stories.

Peace always,

Deirdre x

More from Deirdre Maguire

Books:

My On Purpose Planner

Workshops and Seminars:

Personal Power and Transformation Weekend

The Powerhouse of Peace Self-Mastery Program

Practitioner Mentoring:

Secrets of a Faster Master – live and online practitioner mentoring courses.

For more information, visit:

www.deirdremaguire.com

PHP Self Mastery Pillars of Truth

1. I am the Expression of Life.
2. You are the Expression of Life.
3. We are all One.
4. Life Source has got my back – always.
5. I am safe.
6. I belong.
7. I serve.

- *From The Powerhouse of Peace Self Mastery Program™*

Printed in Great Britain
by Amazon